# THE ALTERNATIVE EGG COOKBOOK

# THE ALTERNATIVE EGG COOKBOOK

All your favourite recipes using
pasteurised dried and frozen egg

## Frances Naldrett

foulsham

LONDON • NEW YORK • TORONTO • SYDNEY

# foulsham

Yeovil Road, Slough, Berkshire SL1 4JH

ISBN 0–572–01570–4

Copyright © 1989   Frances Naldrett

Printed in Great Britain at The Bath Press, Avon

# CONTENTS

# INTRODUCTION

Eggs are the original pre-packed convenience food. No family's weekly shopping list was complete without them: to be fried, poached or soft boiled for breakfast, scrambled or in an omelette for a light lunch or supper, or as the basic ingredient in a large number of rich and delicious desserts and dinner party dishes. From time to time we were told not to eat too many of them, but to anyone who had young children or an elderly relative to care for, eggs were the always available, easily digested answer to a quick meal.

Suddenly, in the autumn of 1988, this invaluable standby was labelled as dangerous to health, particularly for the very people to whom they had been of most convenience. And this was not a scare which was quickly dispelled. The production line for this convenience food could not be closed down overnight, the machinery sterilised and production started again a few days later. This was a problem which would take a number of years to combat.

Of course the chances of a healthy person being seriously affected by *salmonella enteritidis*, the strain associated with eggs and poultry, are slight, but nevertheless the Government's Chief Medical Officers have recommended that for the foreseeable future no one should eat uncooked eggs, and that the young, the elderly and anyone with a health problem should avoid eating lightly cooked eggs, too.

Having looked after my elderly mother for a number of years I know that the dishes she liked best contained eggs, and very often the dish would not be cooked in accordance with current government guidelines. These include simple recipes like Tomato Scramble. Home-made Mayonnaise, Duchesse Potatoes, Omelettes, Meringues and everybody's favourite dessert, Chocolate Pots. The thought that dishes like these would have to be banished for ever set me experimenting with the dried and frozen egg products available; somewhat reluctantly at first, as I am old enough to remember, just, the reputation dried eggs had in the war years! After trying out a few recipes, however, my enthusiasm grew, and my success was crowned when I served two popular desserts – Crême Brulée and the above-mentioned Chocolate Pots – to my critical gourmet other half who refused to believe that I had used dried egg. As my experiments progressed I became more confident in the recipes I tried and found that such classics as Mayonnaise and Hollandaise Sauce could be made successfully.

I do not guarantee that someone with acutely sensitive taste buds will not be able to detect the flavour of dried egg in some of the more delicate recipes, but I have found that often this may be detectable when the recipe is first made, but once the flavours have matured any slight taste of dried egg disappears. This is particularly the case with Lemon Curd. In fact I have been so pleased with the results that I shall continue to use dried egg in many of these recipes even after the 'all clear'!

Frozen pasteurised eggs are stocked by some supermarkets and freezer centres and I have used these in scrambled egg dishes, omelettes and some sauces, where I do not think that dried eggs give acceptable results.

During the weeks I was testing these recipes, there was no saving in cost in using dried or frozen eggs in comparison to fresh eggs. However, as dried egg white can be used for meringues and some soufflés you are not left with a lot of egg yolks over; and dried egg, although containing the white as well, is still perfect for recipes which normally only use egg yolks. In fact dried egg was slightly more expensive, but well worth the extra cost for peace of mind.

I have included a chapter on basic recipes, where the egg is cooked sufficiently to be perfectly safe, for interest and for emergencies, so that you can whip up a cake or some éclairs, or a Yorkshire pud to accompany the joint even if you run out of fresh eggs.

I have not set out to be particularly adventurous in the choice of recipes I have included in this book; my aim is to show how everyday recipes can still be enjoyed. Inevitably the largest chapter is the one on desserts, as these are where eggs are used either uncooked or partially cooked to the greatest extent. Here my problem was to choose the widest range of dishes to show how recipes can be adapted so that you can experiment with your own particular favourites and achieve good results using pasteurised egg, either frozen or dried. You will find recipes as humble as Bread and Butter Pudding, as popular as Cold Lemon Soufflé and as rich and delicious as St Emilion.

I hope you will find in *The Alternative Egg Cookbook* some of your own favourite recipes, and others less familiar to you will be added to your cookery repertoire.

# ABOUT THE RECIPES

## Ingredients

***Dried Egg Powder:*** There are several brands of dried egg, some available from health food shops, others from camping suppliers, but I have found the most widely available is the Supercook brand which most large supermarkets stock. In most recipes I found it best to mix the dried egg with water before adding to other ingredients, and I varied the amount of water according to each particular recipe. A small wire whisk is the best utensil to use for mixing it to a smooth cream.

***Dried Egg White:*** There are two main brands: Supercook and Meri-white. The Supercook egg white is packed in a small drum and you measure out the quantity called for. It is easiest if you mix an equal quantity of egg white powder and water until the egg white has dissolved, then add the remaining water. The Meri-white product is already measured in envelopes, but one envelope can replace 15 ml/1 tbls in the recipes. Egg albumin used in cake icing is, in fact, dried egg white and is available from specialist cake decorating shops. Dissolve the albumin in the same amount of water called for in the recipes.

***Frozen Pasteurised Egg:*** This product is packed in cartons and is available from some supermarkets and freezer centres. It is the whole egg beaten, so can replace eggs in any recipe, but not, of course, if the eggs are separated. It is recommended that it is left to thaw in the refrigerator for 24 hours and that once thawed it is used within 3 days. I found it particularly good for omelettes and scrambled egg dishes.

## Method Techniques

Dried egg, when used in recipes such as Hollandaise Sauce and egg custards, may curdle, just as fresh egg does. Care must therefore be taken when making this type of recipe. A number of the desserts have a custard base. In the method I have given instructions for making this in a saucepan over a low heat, but if the custard gets too hot or boils it will curdle, so if preferred the mixture can be cooked in a bowl over a pan of boiling water. This will take longer but reduce the risk of it curdling.

Dried egg white whisks up well, but do make sure that the bowl and whisk are absolutely clean; just a touch of grease will prevent the egg white whisking stiffly. If possible use an electric mixer. A small deep bowl is better than a large shallow one, particularly when only a small quantity of egg white is being whisked. Use the egg white as quickly as possible after it has been whisked stiffly. When whisked sufficiently, you should be able to turn the bowl upside-down without the egg white falling out!

A slotted draining spoon is the ideal utensil for folding whisked egg whites into other mixtures.

This is not intended to be a book on microwave cooking, but where appropriate I have included microwave cooking notes, and anyone who owns a microwave oven and has a little experience will soon be able to adapt many of the recipes to cook in this way.

# STARTERS AND SNACKS

Eggs are the main ingredient of a number of popular starters, and egg dishes are a great standby for quick snacks. This chapter includes a selection of hot and cold starters and tasty snacks, some light and others more substantial, suitable for all occasions from a light lunch to a late night supper.

# Cream of Watercress Soup

Serves 4

|  | Metric | Imperial | American |
|---|---|---|---|
| Bunch of watercress | 1 | 1 | 1 |
| Medium potatoes | 2 | 2 | 2 |
| Butter | 50 g | 2 oz | $\frac{1}{4}$ cup |
| Chicken stock | 900 ml | $1\frac{1}{2}$ pt | $3\frac{3}{4}$ cups |
| Milk | 275 ml | $\frac{1}{2}$ pt | $1\frac{1}{4}$ cups |
| Salt and pepper |  |  |  |
| Dried egg powder | 45 ml | 3 tbls | 3 tbls |
| Water | 45 ml | 3 tbls | 3 tbls |
| Single cream | 150 ml | $\frac{1}{4}$ pt | $\frac{2}{3}$ cup |

1. Wash the watercress thoroughly, reserve a few small sprigs for garnish and roughly chop the remainder. Peel and slice the potatoes.

2. Melt the butter in a large saucepan, add the watercress and cook over a low heat for 3 minutes. Add the potatoes and stock. Bring to the boil, cover and simmer for 20 minutes or until the potatoes are tender.

3. Purée the soup in a blender or food processor, then return it to the pan. Add the milk and seasoning and bring just to the boil.

4. Blend the dried egg and water to a smooth paste, stir in the cream. Whisk the egg mixture into the hot soup and reheat gently, but do not allow to boil. Serve in warm soup bowls garnished with reserved watercress sprigs and a swirl of cream, if liked.

## Variations

***Cream of Lettuce Soup:***   Replace the watercress with half a round lettuce.

***Cream of Spinach Soup:***   Replace the watercress with 450 g/1 lb of fresh spinach or 225 g/8 oz of chopped frozen spinach. Add a little grated nutmeg to the finished soup.

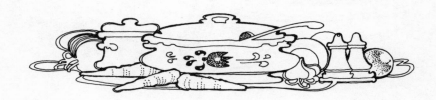

# Avgolemono

Serves 4

|  | Metric | Imperial | American |
| --- | --- | --- | --- |
| Butter | 25 g | 1 oz | 2 tbls |
| Plain flour | 25 g | 1 oz | $\frac{1}{4}$ cup |
| Chicken stock | 550 ml | 1 pt | $2\frac{1}{2}$ cups |
| Cooked rice (optional) | 50 g | 2 oz | $\frac{1}{2}$ cup |
| Dried egg powder | 30 ml | 2 tbls | 2 tbls |
| Water | 30 ml | 2 tbls | 2 tbls |
| Lemon juice | 45 ml | 3 tbls | 3 tbls |
| Salt and pepper |  |  |  |
| Chopped parsley | 30 ml | 2 tbls | 2 tbls |

1. Melt the butter in a large saucepan, add the flour and cook for 1 minute. Gradually blend in the chicken stock. Bring to the boil and simmer for 5 minutes. Add the rice, if using.

2. Blend the dried egg, water and lemon juice until smooth. Stir into the hot stock a little at a time. Heat the soup, but do not allow it to boil. Season it to taste. The soup should be smooth. Serve hot sprinkled with chopped parsley.

# Creamed Mushroom Soup

Serves 4

|  | Metric | Imperial | American |
| --- | --- | --- | --- |
| Button mushrooms | 175 g | 6 oz | 6 oz |
| Medium onion | 1 | 1 | 1 |
| Butter or margarine | 25 g | 1 oz | 2 tbls |
| Plain flour | 25 g | 1 oz | $\frac{1}{4}$ cup |
| Chicken stock | 750 ml | $1\frac{1}{4}$ pt | 3 cups |
| Milk | 275 ml | $\frac{1}{2}$ pt | $1\frac{1}{4}$ cups |
| Salt and pepper |  |  |  |
| Dried egg powder | 45 ml | 3 tbls | 3 tbls |
| Water | 75 ml | 5 tbls | 5 tbls |
| Single cream | 150 ml | $\frac{1}{4}$ pt | $\frac{2}{3}$ cup |
| Chopped parsley | 15 ml | 1 tbls | 1 tbls |

**1.** Slice the mushrooms and onion. Melt the butter or margarine in a saucepan, add the mushrooms and onion and cook gently until tender. Stir in the flour and cook for 1 minute.

**2.** Gradually stir in the stock and bring to the boil. Simmer for 10 minutes until the vegetables are tender. Purée in a blender or food processor.

**3.** Return the soup to the rinsed-out pan, add the milk and season with salt and pepper. Bring to the boil.

**4.** Meanwhile mix the dried egg powder and water to a smooth paste, then blend in the cream. Stir into the soup and heat gently but do not boil. Serve the soup sprinkled with chopped parsley.

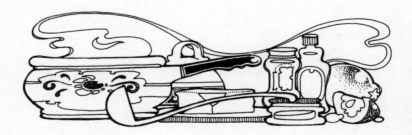

# Creamed Fish Scallops

Serves 4

|  | Metric | Imperial | American |
|---|---|---|---|
| Monkfish | 225 g | 8 oz | $\frac{1}{2}$ lb |
| Salt | 2.5 ml | $\frac{1}{2}$ tsp | $\frac{1}{2}$ tsp |
| Dried egg powder | 30 ml | 2 tbls | 2 tbls |
| Water | 60 ml | 4 tbls | 4 tbls |
| Single cream | 150 ml | $\frac{1}{4}$ pt | $\frac{2}{3}$ cup |
| Chopped parsley | 15 ml | 1 tbls | 1 tbls |
| Salt and pepper |  |  |  |
| Browned breadcrumbs | 30 ml | 2 tbls | 2 tbls |
| Butter | 25 g | 1 oz | 2 tbls |

1. Remove any skin and the centre bone from the monkfish. Place in a saucepan with the salt, just cover with water and bring slowly to the boil. Reduce the heat and poach the fish very gently until tender, about 5 minutes.

2. Cut the fish into small cubes and divide between 4 scallop shells or small ramekins.

3. Mix the dried egg powder and water to a smooth cream and add the cream and parsley. Season with salt and pepper. Heat very gently, stirring until the sauce thickens slightly. Do not allow to boil. Pour over the fish in the dishes.

4. Sprinkle each dish with breadcrumbs and dot with butter. Brown under a hot grill. Serve at once.

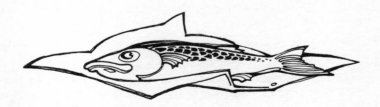

# Salmon Mousse

Serves 6

|  | Metric | Imperial | American |
|---|---|---|---|
| Butter | 25 g | 1 oz | 2 tbls |
| Plain flour | 25 g | 1 oz | $\frac{1}{4}$ cup |
| Mustard powder | 2.5 ml | $\frac{1}{2}$ tsp | $\frac{1}{2}$ tsp |
| Salt | 5 ml | 1 tsp | 1 tsp |
| Caster sugar | 2.5 ml | $\frac{1}{2}$ tsp | $\frac{1}{2}$ tsp |
| Cayenne pepper |  |  |  |
| Paprika | 5 ml | 1 tsp | 1 tsp |
| Milk | 150 ml | $\frac{1}{4}$ pt | $\frac{2}{3}$ cup |
| Dried egg powder | 30 ml | 2 tbls | 2 tbls |
| Water | 60 ml | 4 tbls | 4 tbls |
| Envelope of gelatine | 1 | 1 | 1 |
| White wine vinegar | 15 ml | 1 tbls | 1 tbls |
| Can red salmon (212 g/7 oz) | 1 | 1 | 1 |
| Dried egg white | 30 ml | 2 tbls | 2 tbls |
| Water | 120 ml | 8 tbls | 8 tbls |
| Whipping cream | 150 ml | $\frac{1}{4}$ pt | $\frac{2}{3}$ cup |
| Lemon to garnish |  |  |  |
| Fresh fennel to garnish |  |  |  |

1. Melt the butter in a saucepan, stir in the flour and cook for 1 minute, stirring. Remove from the heat and stir in the mustard, salt, sugar, a pinch of cayenne and the paprika.

2. Gradually blend in the milk, return to the heat and bring to the boil, stirring continuously. Simmer for 2 minutes.

3. Blend the egg powder and water together to make a smooth paste. Stir into the sauce.

4. Sprinkle the gelatine over the vinegar in a small bowl. Add the liquid from the can of salmon and mix well. Place the bowl in a pan of hot, but not boiling water and stir occasionally until the gelatine has dissolved. (Alternatively place the bowl in a microwave oven on DEFROST setting until the gelatine has dissolved.) Stir into the sauce and leave to cool, but not set.

5. Remove the skin and bones from the salmon, flake the fish and stir into the sauce.

6. Place the egg white in a basin, gradually blend in 30 ml/2 tbls of the water until smooth, then stir in the remaining water. Whisk until very stiff. Whisk the cream until it holds its shape. Fold the egg white and cream into the salmon mixture and turn into 6 small ramekin dishes. Chill until firm. Garnish with a twist of lemon and small sprig of fresh fennel and serve with melba toast or salad.

# Prawn Cocktail

Serves 4

|                              | Metric  | Imperial       | American          |
| ---------------------------- | ------- | -------------- | ----------------- |
| Dried egg powder             | 30 ml   | 2 tbls         | 2 tbls            |
| Lemon juice                  | 45 ml   | 3 tbls         | 3 tbls            |
| Corn oil                     | 150 ml  | $\frac{1}{4}$ pt | $\frac{2}{3}$ cup |
| Tomato ketchup               | 30 ml   | 2 tbls         | 2 tbls            |
| Single cream                 | 30 ml   | 2 tbls         | 2 tbls            |
| Salt and pepper              |         |                |                   |
| Crisp lettuce                |         |                |                   |
| Cooked, shelled prawns       | 225 g   | 8 oz           | $\frac{1}{2}$ lb  |
| Lemon wedges                 | 4       | 4              | 4                 |
| Unshelled prawns (optional)  | 4       | 4              | 4                 |

1. Place the dried egg in a basin and blend in 30 ml/2 tbls of lemon juice. Gradually blend in the oil, a few drops at a time, whisking with a wire whisk. As the mixture thickens the oil may be added more quickly. Add the remaining lemon juice when half the oil has been added.

2. When all the oil has been added and the mayonnaise is thick and smooth, whisk in the tomato ketchup and single cream. Season to taste.

3. Shred the lettuce finely and place in 4 individual glasses. Divide the prawns between the glasses and spoon over the sauce. Decorate each glass with a wedge of lemon and a whole prawn, if liked.

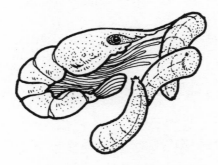

# Coquilles St Jacques Bonne Femme

Serves 4 as a starter, 2 as a main course

|  | Metric | Imperial | American |
| --- | --- | --- | --- |
| *Duchesse potatoes (see page 48)* | | | |
| *Large scallops* | *4* | *4* | *4* |
| *Dry cider* | *150 ml* | *$\frac{1}{4}$ pt* | *$\frac{2}{3}$ cups* |
| *Carrot* | *1* | *1* | *1* |
| *Onion* | *1* | *1* | *1* |
| *Bay leaf* | *1* | *1* | *1* |
| *Mushrooms* | *75 g* | *3 oz* | *3 oz* |
| *Butter* | *25 g* | *1 oz* | *2 tbls* |
| *Plain flour* | *15 ml* | *1 tbls* | *1 tbls* |
| *Dried egg powder* | *30 ml* | *2 tbls* | *2 tbls* |
| *Water* | *45 ml* | *3 tbls* | *3 tbls* |
| *Single cream* | *150 ml* | *$\frac{1}{4}$ pt* | *$\frac{2}{3}$ cup* |
| *Salt and pepper* | | | |

1. Pipe the Duchesse potatoes around the edge of 4 scallop shells or individual gratin dishes. (Two dishes for a main course.)

2. Wash the scallops and place in a saucepan with the cider. Peel and slice the carrot and onion and add to the saucepan with the bay leaf. Bring to simmering point and poach the scallops for 8 to 10 minutes until tender.

3. Wipe and slice the mushrooms. Melt the butter in a saucepan, add the mushrooms and cook without browning for about 4 minutes. Stir in the flour and cook for 1 minute. Strain the liquid from the scallops and stir into the flour mixture. Bring to the boil. Cook for 2 minutes, stirring continuously. Quarter the scallops and add to the sauce.

4. Blend the dried egg and water to a smooth cream. Stir in the single cream. Add to the sauce and reheat, without boiling. Season with salt and pepper. Divide between the potato-edged dishes.

5. Place the dishes under a medium grill to brown the potato edge. Serve hot.

## Variation

***Monkfish Scallops:*** Replace the scallops with 225 g/8 oz monkfish cut into cubes.

# Cheese Aigrettes

Makes 16

|  | Metric | Imperial | American |
|---|---|---|---|
| Plain flour | 50 g | 2 oz | $\frac{1}{2}$ cup |
| Salt | | | |
| Butter | 25 g | 1 oz | 2 tbls |
| Water | 150 ml | $\frac{1}{4}$ pt | $\frac{2}{3}$ cup |
| Frozen pasteurised egg, thawed | 50 ml | 2 fl oz | $\frac{1}{4}$ cup |
| Cheddar cheese, grated | 100 g | 4 oz | 1 cup |
| Cayenne pepper | | | |
| Oil for deep frying | | | |

1. Sift the flour and a pinch of salt on to a sheet of greaseproof paper. Put the butter and water into a pan and heat gently until the butter melts. Bring to the boil. Remove from the heat and pour in the flour. Return to a low heat and beat until the mixture is smooth and leaves the sides of the pan. Cool slightly.

2. Add the egg gradually, beating well between each addition. When all the egg has been added, the mixture should be glossy and smooth. Beat in the cheese and a pinch of cayenne pepper.

3. Heat the oil in a deep fat fryer to 190°C/375°F or until a cube of day-old bread browns in 30 seconds. Drop teaspoonsful of the cheese mixture into the hot fat, about 6 at a time, and fry for about 5 minutes until puffed and golden brown. Lift out with a draining spoon and drain on kitchen paper. Keep warm. Serve sprinkled with a little extra grated cheese, if liked.

# French Toast

Serves 4

|                                    | Metric  | Imperial          | American            |
|------------------------------------|---------|-------------------|---------------------|
| Frozen pasteurised egg, thawed     | 75 ml   | 3 tbls            | 3 tbls              |
| Milk                               | 150 ml  | $\frac{1}{4}$ pt  | $\frac{2}{3}$ cup   |
| Salt and pepper                    |         |                   |                     |
| Thick slices white bread           | 4       | 4                 | 4                   |
| Butter or oil for frying           |         |                   |                     |

1. Whisk the egg and milk together and season with salt and pepper.

2. Pour into a shallow dish and dip each slice of the bread in the egg mixture, making sure each side is coated.

3. Heat the butter or oil in a frying pan and fry the slices of bread until golden on each side. Serve hot topped with crisply grilled bacon rashers.

## Variation

***Cinnamon Toasts:***    Omit the seasoning from the egg mixture and sprinkle the cooked toasts with 5 ml/1 tsp of cinnamon powder mixed with 15 ml/1 tbls of caster sugar.

# Spanish Omelette

Serves 2

|  | Metric | Imperial | American |
|---|---|---|---|
| Potatoes | 350 g | 12 oz | $\frac{3}{4}$ lb |
| Onions | 225 g | 8 oz | $\frac{1}{2}$ lb |
| Olive oil | 60 ml | 4 tbls | 4 tbls |
| Cooked peas | 100 g | 4 oz | $\frac{3}{4}$ cup |
| Salt and pepper | | | |
| Frozen pasteurised egg, thawed | 175 ml | 6 fl oz | $\frac{3}{4}$ cup |
| Water | 30 ml | 2 tbls | 2 tbls |

1. Scrub the potatoes, then cook them in boiling salted water for 10 minutes. Peel, then cut into 2 cm/$\frac{3}{4}$ in cubes. Peel and coarsely chop the onions.

2. Heat the oil in a frying pan, add the potatoes and onion and stir to coat in the oil. Cover with a lid and cook gently, stirring occasionally, until the vegetables are soft. Add the peas and season to taste.

3. Beat the egg and water together, then pour the egg mixture over the vegetables and cook the omelette, shaking the pan from time to time to prevent sticking, until golden brown underneath. Place the pan under a medium grill to set the top of the omelette. Serve cut into wedges, with salad as accompaniment.

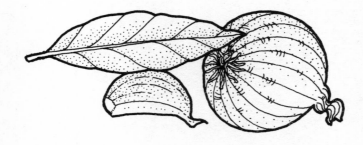

# Savoury Omelette

Serves 1

|                                      | Metric  | Imperial          | American          |
| ------------------------------------ | ------- | ----------------- | ----------------- |
| *Frozen pasteurised egg, thawed*     | *150 ml* | $\frac{1}{4}$ *pt* | $\frac{2}{3}$ *cup* |
| *Salt and pepper*                    |         |                   |                   |
| *Water*                              | *15 ml* | *1 tbls*          | *1 tbls*          |
| *Butter*                             | *15 g*  | $\frac{1}{2}$ *oz* | *1 tbls*          |
| *Filling (see below)*                |         |                   |                   |

1. Beat the egg, seasoning and water together. Heat the butter in a small frying pan or omelette pan until hot, but not brown.

2. Pour in the egg mixture, leave for a few seconds, then lift the egg from the sides of the pan towards the centre, as it sets, letting the uncooked mixture run to the sides of the pan. Leave over the heat until the bottom of the omelette is golden brown and the top almost set.

3. Add the filling, then fold the omelette in half and slide out of the pan onto a warm plate.

## Fillings

*Mushroom:*   Fry 50 g/2 oz of finely sliced mushrooms in a little butter.

*Prawn:*   Heat 50 g/2 oz of shelled prawns in a little butter.

*Cheese:*   Grate 50 g/2 oz of strong-flavoured hard cheese into the omelette.

*Herb:*   Add 15 ml/1 tbls of chopped, fresh herbs to the beaten eggs before pouring into the pan.

*Ham:*   Add 50 g/2 oz of finely chopped ham to the eggs before pouring into the pan.

# Piperade

Serves 4

|  | Metric | Imperial | American |
|---|---|---|---|
| Green pepper | 1 | 1 | 1 |
| Red pepper | 1 | 1 | 1 |
| Tomatoes | 450 g | 1 lb | 1 lb |
| Onions | 2 | 2 | 2 |
| Garlic clove | 1 | 1 | 1 |
| Butter | 50 g | 2 oz | $\frac{1}{4}$ cup |
| Frozen pasteurised egg, thawed | 275 ml | $\frac{1}{2}$ pt | $1\frac{1}{4}$ cups |
| Chopped fresh basil (optional) | 15 ml | 1 tbls | 1 tbls |
| Salt and pepper | | | |
| Milk | 45 ml | 3 tbls | 3 tbls |
| Bacon rashers, grilled | 8 | 8 | 8 |

**1.** Cut the peppers in half, discard the seeds and cores and slice into thin strips. Skin and chop the tomatoes. Peel and thinly slice the onions. Peel and crush the garlic.

**2.** Heat the butter in a large pan. Add the peppers and onions and fry gently for 5 minutes. Add the tomatoes and garlic and cook for a further 5 minutes until all the vegetables are soft.

**3.** Beat the egg, basil, seasoning and milk together. Pour over the vegetables and cook gently, stirring, until the eggs are lightly scrambled. Serve topped with bacon rashers.

# Crispy Cheese Pancakes

Serves 4

|  | Metric | Imperial | American |
|---|---|---|---|
| **Pancakes** | | | |
| Plain flour | 100 g | 4 oz | 1 cup |
| Dried egg powder | 30 ml | 2 tbls | 2 tbls |
| Milk | 275 ml | $\frac{1}{2}$ pt | $1\frac{1}{4}$ cups |
| Water | 60 ml | 4 tbls | 4 tbls |
| Oil for frying | | | |
| **Filling** | | | |
| Curd cheese | 225 g | 8 oz | 1 cup |
| Cheddar cheese, grated | 100 g | 4 oz | 1 cup |
| Dried egg powder | 30 ml | 2 tbls | 2 tbls |
| Water | 60 ml | 4 tbls | 4 tbls |
| Dried thyme | 5 ml | 1 tsp | 1 tsp |
| Salt and pepper | | | |
| Butter | 50 g | 2 oz | $\frac{1}{4}$ cup |

1. Sift the flour and dried egg into a bowl. Gradually blend in the milk to make a smooth batter. Stir in the water.

2. Heat a little oil in a small frying pan, then pour off into a jug to leave the pan lightly greased. Pour in sufficient batter to coat the pan thinly. Cook until golden brown on the bottom. Turn the pancake out of the pan. Make 7 more pancakes in the same way, cooking on one side only.

3. Mix the curd and Cheddar cheeses together. Blend the dried egg and water to a smooth cream and stir into the cheeses with the thyme and seasoning.

4. Place a spoonful of cheese mixture on the cooked side of a pancake, fold the edges of the pancake over to enclose the filling completely. Repeat with the remaining pancakes and filling.

5. Melt half the butter in a large frying pan, put in 4 pancakes, join underneath and fry until golden. Turn and fry on the other side. Remove from the pan and drain on kitchen paper. Fry the remaining pancakes in the same way, using the remaining butter. Serve hot.

# Scrambled Eggs

Serves 2

|  | Metric | Imperial | American |
| --- | --- | --- | --- |
| Frozen pasteurised egg, thawed | 150 ml | $\frac{1}{4}$ pt | $\frac{2}{3}$ cup |
| Milk | 60 ml | 4 tbls | 4 tbls |
| Salt and pepper |  |  |  |
| Butter | 25 g | 1 oz | 2 tbls |
| Hot buttered toast |  |  |  |

1. Beat the egg and milk together and season with salt and pepper.

2. Melt the butter in a small saucepan, add the egg mixture and stir over a low heat until the egg is lightly scrambled.

3. Divide the egg between two pieces of hot buttered toast.

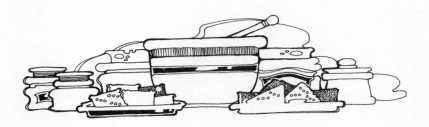

# Tomato Scramble

Serves 2

|  | Metric | Imperial | American |
|---|---|---|---|
| Tomatoes | 2 | 2 | 2 |
| Frozen pasteurised egg, thawed | 150 ml | $\frac{1}{4}$ pt | $\frac{2}{3}$ cup |
| Salt and pepper | | | |
| Chopped fresh basil or marjoram | 15 ml | 1 tbls | 1 tbls |
| Butter | 25 g | 1 oz | 2 tbls |
| Muffins | 2 | 2 | 2 |

1. Place the tomatoes in a basin, cover with boiling water, leave for 30 seconds, then drain and remove the skins. Cut the tomatoes in halves and scoop out the seeds. Finally chop the tomato flesh.

2. Season the egg with salt and pepper, and stir in the herbs. Melt the butter in a saucepan, add the tomato and stir over a low heat for 2 minutes. Add the egg and stir until lightly scrambled.

3. Meanwhile split, toast and butter the muffins. Divide the tomato scramble between the muffin halves and serve hot.

# Scotch Woodcock

Serves 2

|  | Metric | Imperial | American |
|---|---|---|---|
| Anchovy fillets | 4 | 4 | 4 |
| Frozen pasteurised egg, thawed | 150 ml | $\frac{1}{4}$ pt | $\frac{2}{3}$ cup |
| Salt and pepper | | | |
| Milk | 30 ml | 2 tbls | 2 tbls |
| Butter | 25 g | 1 oz | 2 tbls |
| Capers | 8 | 8 | 8 |
| Buttered toast slices | 2 | 2 | 2 |

**1.** Cut two anchovy fillets in half lengthways and reserve. Finely chop the remaining anchovies, and add to the egg with the salt, pepper and milk. Mix well.

**2.** Melt the butter in a small saucepan, add the egg mixture and stir over a low heat until lightly scrambled. Stir in the capers.

**3.** Divide the egg between the slices of toast and arrange halved anchovy fillets in a cross on each portion. Serve hot.

# Cheese Boats

Serves 4

|  | Metric | Imperial | American |
| --- | --- | --- | --- |
| **Pastry** | | | |
| Plain flour | 100 g | 4 oz | 1 cup |
| Salt | | | |
| Butter or margarine | 25 g | 1 oz | 2 tbls |
| Lard | 25 g | 1 oz | 2 tbls |
| Cold water | 15 ml | 3 tsp | 3 tsp |
| **Filling** | | | |
| Red Leicester cheese, grated | 100 g | 4 oz | 1 cup |
| Soft white breadcrumbs | 50 g | 2 oz | 1 cup |
| Melted butter | 30 ml | 2 tbls | 2 tbls |
| Dried egg powder | 15 ml | 1 tbls | 1 tbls |
| Water | 15 ml | 1 tbls | 1 tbls |
| Milk | 15 ml | 1 tbls | 1 tbls |
| Salt | | | |
| Cayenne pepper | | | |
| Chopped parsley | | | |

1. Sift the flour and a pinch of salt into a bowl. Add the fats cut into small pieces and rub in with the fingertips until the mixture resembles fine breadcrumbs. Add about 3 teaspoons of water and mix to form a firm dough.

2. Knead the pastry lightly, then roll out on a floured board and use to line 8 boat-shaped tins or 8 tartlet tins. Place on a baking sheet, prick the bases well and cook in the centre of a moderately hot oven at 200°C/400°F/Gas mark 6 for about 12 minutes, until pale brown.

3. Mix the cheese and breadcrumbs together. Stir in the melted butter. Mix the dried egg, water and milk to a smooth cream. Stir into the cheese mixture and season to taste with salt and cayenne pepper.

4. Divide the cheese mixture between the pastry boats and heat in a moderate oven at 180°C/350°F/Gas mark 4 for 15 minutes. Sprinkle with chopped parsley and serve warm.

# Ratatouille Soufflés

Serves 4

| | Metric | Imperial | American |
|---|---|---|---|
| Ratatouille (390 g/14 oz can) | 1 | 1 | 1 |
| Butter | 25 g | 1 oz | 2 tbls |
| Plain flour | 25 g | 1 oz | $\frac{1}{4}$ cup |
| Milk | 150 ml | $\frac{1}{4}$ pt | $\frac{2}{3}$ cup |
| Cheddar cheese, grated | 75 g | 3 oz | $\frac{3}{4}$ cup |
| Dried egg powder | 45 ml | 3 tbls | 3 tbls |
| Water | 45 ml | 3 tbls | 3 tbls |
| Salt | 5 ml | 1 tsp | 1 tsp |
| Cayenne pepper | | | |
| Dried egg white | 25 ml | $1\frac{1}{2}$ tbls | $1\frac{1}{2}$ tbls |
| Water | 90 ml | 6 tbls | 6 tbls |

1. Butter 4 large ramekin dishes. Divide the ratatouille between the dishes.

2. Melt the butter in a saucepan, stir in the flour and cook for 1 minute. Remove from the heat and blend in the milk. Return to the heat and bring to the boil, stirring. Cook for 2 minutes. Stir in the cheese.

3. Blend the dried egg and the 45 ml/3 tbls of water to a smooth paste, stir into the sauce and mix well. Season with salt and cayenne pepper.

4. Blend the dried egg white and 30 ml/2 tbls of water to a smooth paste, then gradually stir in the remaining water. Whisk until stiff. Fold a spoonful into the cheese mixture, then fold the cheese mixture into the whisked egg white with a metal spoon, quickly and lightly. Divide between the ramekin dishes.

5. Cook in a moderately hot oven at 200°C/400°F/Gas mark 6 until well risen and golden brown, about 20 minutes. Serve at once.

# MAIN DISHES

It is surprising how many favourite recipes include eggs to add richness or thicken the sauce, or even as the main ingredient. Many of them include well-cooked eggs, but in some the egg is added just before the dish is finished, and with others the cooking time is too short to ensure that the eggs are sufficiently cooked.

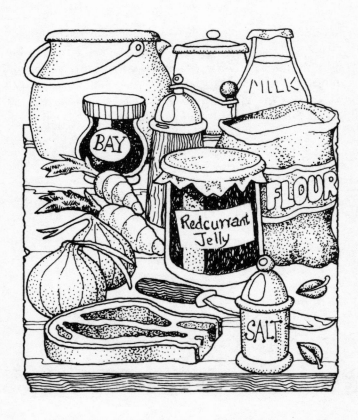

# Plaice Veronique

Serves 4

|  | Metric | Imperial | American |
| --- | --- | --- | --- |
| *Plaice fillets* | *8* | *8* | *8* |
| *Salt and pepper* | | | |
| *Seedless white grapes* | *100 g* | *4 oz* | *$\frac{1}{4}$ lb* |
| *Dry white wine* | *150 ml* | *$\frac{1}{4}$ pt* | *$\frac{2}{3}$ cup* |
| *Milk* | *150 ml* | *$\frac{1}{4}$ pt* | *$\frac{2}{3}$ cup* |
| *Butter* | *25 g* | *1 oz* | *2 tbls* |
| *Plain flour* | *25 g* | *1 oz* | *$\frac{1}{4}$ cup* |
| *Dried egg powder* | *15 ml* | *1 tbls* | *1 tbls* |
| *Water* | *30 ml* | *2 tbls* | *2 tbls* |
| *Single cream* | *150 ml* | *$\frac{1}{4}$ pt* | *$\frac{2}{3}$ cup* |
| *Sprigs of parsley to garnish* | | | |

**1.** Remove any dark skin from the plaice fillets and lay all the fillets skin or skinned side up on a board. Season with salt and pepper. Place a few grapes on each fillet and fold the fillets in three, enclosing the grapes. Place in an ovenproof dish. Pour over the wine and cover with foil. Reserve the remaining grapes for garnish.

**2.** Cook in a moderate oven at 180°C/350°F/Gas mark 4 for 12 to 15 minutes. (Alternatively cover the dish with microwave cling film and cook on **HIGH** for 6 minutes.)

**3.** When the fish is cooked, lift the fillets on to a serving dish and keep warm. Strain the liquid into a jug and add the milk.

**4.** Melt the butter in a saucepan, stir in the flour and cook for 1 minute. Gradually blend in the milk mixture and bring to the boil, stirring. Cook for 2 minutes, stirring. Remove from the heat.

**5.** Blend the egg powder and water to make a smooth paste, stir in the cream. Stir into the sauce and reheat gently, without boiling. Pour over the fish fillets and garnish with the reserved grapes and sprigs of parsley.

# Fish Cakes

Makes 6

|  | Metric | Imperial | American |
|---|---|---|---|
| Cod or haddock | 350 g | 12 oz | $\frac{3}{4}$ lb |
| Potatoes | 350 g | 12 oz | $\frac{3}{4}$ lb |
| Butter or margarine | 25 g | 1 oz | 2 tbls |
| Chopped parsley | 60 ml | 2 tbls | 2 tbls |
| Salt and pepper |  |  |  |
| Dried egg powder | 60 ml | 4 tbls | 4 tbls |
| Water | 90 ml | 6 tbls | 6 tbls |
| Fine fresh breadcrumbs | 50 g | 2 oz | 1 cup |
| Oil or fat for frying |  |  |  |
| Lemon wedges to serve |  |  |  |

**1.** Poach the fish in salted water until it flakes easily with a fork, about 8 minutes. (Alternatively, place in a shallow dish with a little water, cover with microwave cling film and microwave on HIGH until cooked, about 4 minutes.)

**2.** Peel and cut up the potatoes and cook in boiling salted water until tender. Drain and mash smoothly. Stir in the butter or margarine and the parsley. Season well with salt and pepper.

**3.** Flake the fish, discarding the skin and bones. Add to the potato and mix well.

**4.** Blend the dried egg and water to a smooth cream. Stir half into the fish mixture and mix to bind. Turn the mixture on to a floured surface and form into 6 cakes.

**5.** Pour the remaining egg mixture on to a plate. Place the breadcrumbs on another plate and coat the fish cakes first in egg and then in breadcrumbs.

**6.** Heat the oil or fat in a large frying pan and fry the fish cakes until golden on the bottoms, turn and cook on the other sides. Serve piping hot with lemon wedges.

# Kedgeree

Serves 4

|  | Metric | Imperial | American |
|---|---|---|---|
| Long grain rice | 225 g | 8 oz | 1 cup |
| Smoked haddock fillet | 450 g | 1 lb | 1 lb |
| Frozen pasteurised egg, thawed | 90 ml | 6 tbls | 6 tbls |
| Single cream | 90 ml | 6 tbls | 6 tbls |
| Butter or margarine | 100 g | 4 oz | $\frac{1}{2}$ cup |
| Salt and cayenne pepper |  |  |  |
| Grated nutmeg |  |  |  |
| Chopped parsley | 15 ml | 1 tbls | 1 tbls |

1. Cook the rice in plenty of boiling salted water until just tender, about 12 minutes. Drain and rinse with hot water.

2. Poach the haddock fillets in water until the fish flakes easily with a fork, about 10 minutes. (Alternatively place the haddock in a shallow dish with a little water, cover with microwave cling film and microwave on **HIGH** for 5 minutes or until the fish is cooked.)

3. Remove the skin and any bones from the fish, and flake the fish with a fork.

4. Mix the egg and cream. Melt the butter or margarine in a large saucepan, remove from the heat and stir in the haddock, rice and egg mixture. Season with a little salt and cayenne pepper and a pinch of grated nutmeg.

5. Return the pan to the heat and stir over a low heat for about 3 minutes or until heated through. Stir in the parsley. Serve hot.

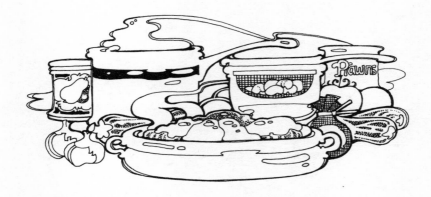

# Omelette Arnold Bennett

Serves 2

|  | Metric | Imperial | American |
|---|---|---|---|
| Butter | 40 g | $1\frac{1}{2}$ oz | 3 tbls |
| Plain flour | 25 g | 1 oz | $\frac{1}{4}$ cup |
| Milk | 275 ml | $\frac{1}{2}$ pt | $1\frac{1}{4}$ cups |
| Cheddar cheese, grated | 75 g | 3 oz | $\frac{3}{4}$ cup |
| Salt and pepper |  |  |  |
| Grated nutmeg |  |  |  |
| Smoked haddock, cooked | 225 g | 8 oz | $\frac{1}{2}$ lb |
| Frozen pasteurised egg, thawed | 250 ml | 8 fl oz | 1 cup |

1. Melt 25 g/1 oz/2 tbls of the butter in a small saucepan, add the flour and cook, stirring, for 2 minutes. Remove from the heat and blend in the milk. Return to the heat and bring to the boil, stirring. Cook for 2 minutes. Stir in 50 g/2 oz/$\frac{1}{2}$ cup of the cheese and season with salt, pepper and a pinch of nutmeg. Keep hot.

2. Flake the haddock with a fork, removing any skin and bones. Lightly whisk the egg and add the haddock. Season with pepper.

3. Heat the remaining butter in an omelette pan, pour in the egg and haddock mixture and cook, lifting the mixture from edges of pan to let the uncooked mixture run underneath. When the omelette is gold underneath but still moist on top, slide on to an ovenproof serving dish and pour over the cheese sauce. Sprinkle with the remaining cheese and brown under a hot grill. Serve at once with crusty bread.

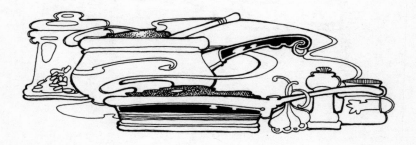

# Chicken with Cashew Nuts

Serves 4

|  | Metric | Imperial | American |
|---|---|---|---|
| Cooked chicken | 350 g | 12 oz | $\frac{3}{4}$ lb |
| Small onion | 1 | 1 | 1 |
| Mushrooms | 50 g | 2 oz | 2 oz |
| Cashew nuts | 50 g | 2 oz | $\frac{1}{3}$ cup |
| Oil | 15 ml | 1 tbls | 1 tbls |
| Butter | 25 g | 1 oz | 2 tbls |
| Cornflour | 10 ml | 2 tsp | 2 tsp |
| Milk | 150 ml | $\frac{1}{4}$ pt | $\frac{2}{3}$ cup |
| Ground ginger | 1.25 ml | $\frac{1}{4}$ tsp | $\frac{1}{4}$ tsp |
| Grated nutmeg | 1.25 ml | $\frac{1}{4}$ tsp | $\frac{1}{4}$ tsp |
| Dried egg powder | 30 ml | 2 tbls | 2 tbls |
| Water | 30 ml | 2 tbls | 2 tbls |
| Natural yoghurt | 150 ml | 5 fl oz | $\frac{2}{3}$ cup |
| Salt and pepper | | | |

1. Cut the chicken into bite-sized pieces. Peel and chop the onion. Wipe and slice the mushrooms.

2. Coarsely chop the cashew nuts, and fry in the oil until golden brown. Drain on kitchen paper.

3. Melt the butter in a medium-sized saucepan. Fry the onion and mushrooms until soft but not browned. Stir in the cornflour and cook for 1 minute. Blend in the milk and cook, stirring, until the sauce comes to the boil. Add the chicken, ginger and nutmeg. Cook for a further 5 minutes.

4. Blend the dried egg and water to a smooth cream, and stir in the yoghurt. Add the yoghurt to the chicken mixture and heat, stirring, but do not allow the sauce to boil. Season to taste, then pour into a warmed serving dish and sprinkle with cashew nuts.

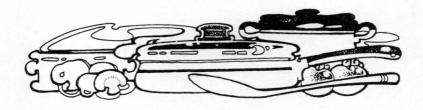

# Chicken Fricassée

Serves 4

|  | Metric | Imperial | American |
|---|---|---|---|
| Chicken joints | 4 | 4 | 4 |
| Onion | 1 | 1 | 1 |
| Cloves | 4 | 4 | 4 |
| Carrots | 2 | 2 | 2 |
| Salt and pepper | | | |
| Bouquet garni | 1 | 1 | 1 |
| Butter | 50 g | 2 oz | $\frac{1}{4}$ cup |
| Plain flour | 50 g | 2 oz | $\frac{1}{2}$ cup |
| Dried egg powder | 30 ml | 2 tbls | 2 tbls |
| Water | 45 ml | 3 tbls | 3 tbls |
| Single cream | 45 ml | 3 tbls | 3 tbls |
| Chopped parsley | | | |
| Grilled bacon rolls | 4 | 4 | 4 |
| Fried bread triangles | 8 | 8 | 8 |

1. Put the chicken joints in a large saucepan. Peel the onion, stick the cloves into the onion and add to the pan. Peel the carrots, cut into pieces and add. Season with salt and pepper. Add the bouqet garni. Just cover the chicken joints with water. Bring to the boil, reduce the heat and simmer until the chicken is cooked, about 1 hour. (Alternatively, cook the chicken in a large casserole in a microwave oven on HIGH for about 25 minutes.)

2. Arrange the chicken joints and carrots in a serving dish and keep them hot. Discard the onion and bouquet garni. Strain 550 ml/1 pt/$2\frac{1}{2}$ cups of the chicken stock and reserve.

3. Melt the butter in a saucepan. Stir in the flour and cook for 2 minutes. Remove from the heat and blend in the reserved chicken stock, bring to the boil and cook for 2 minutes.

4. Blend the dried egg powder and water to a smooth cream, and stir in the single cream. Pour a little of the sauce into the egg mixture. Stir well and then stir into the sauce in the pan. Reheat the sauce without letting it boil. Pour over the chicken in the dish and sprinkle with chopped parsley. Garnish with bacon rolls and fried bread.

# Turkey à la King

Serves 4

|  | Metric | Imperial | American |
| --- | --- | --- | --- |
| Onion | 1 | 1 | 1 |
| Green or red pepper | 1 | 1 | 1 |
| Mushrooms | 100 g | 4 oz | $\frac{1}{4}$ lb |
| Cooked turkey | 350 g | 12 oz | $\frac{3}{4}$ lb |
| Oil | 30 ml | 2 tbls | 2 tbls |
| Dried egg powder | 30 ml | 2 tbls | 2 tbls |
| Water | 30 ml | 2 tbls | 2 tbls |
| Butter | 25 g | 1 oz | 2 tbls |
| Plain flour | 25 g | 1 oz | $\frac{1}{4}$ cup |
| Chicken or turkey stock | 550 ml | 1 pt | $2\frac{1}{2}$ cups |
| Salt and pepper |  |  |  |
| Single cream | 150 ml | $\frac{1}{4}$ pt | $\frac{2}{3}$ cup |
| Chopped parsley | 15 ml | 1 tbls | 1 tbls |

1. Peel and slice the onion. Discard the seeds and core from the pepper, and cut the pepper into thin strips. Wipe and slice the mushrooms. Cut the turkey into bite-sized pieces.

2. Heat the oil and fry the onion over a low heat for 5 minutes. Add the peppers and cook for 3 minutes, add the mushrooms and cook for a further 5 minutes.

3. Blend the dried egg and water to a smooth cream. Melt the butter in a saucepan, add the flour and cook for 2 minutes. Remove from the heat and blend in the stock. Bring to the boil, stirring, and cook for 3 minutes. Stir in the onions, pepper, mushrooms and turkey. Season with salt and pepper. Bring back to the boil and cook gently for about 10 minutes until well heated through.

4. Stir the cream into the egg mixture, then stir this into the turkey mixture and heat for a few minutes, but do not allow to boil. Turn into a warmed serving dish and sprinkle with parsley. Serve with mashed potatoes or rice and a green vegetable.

# Toad-in-the-Hole

Serves 4

|  | Metric | Imperial | American |
| --- | --- | --- | --- |
| Plain flour | 100 g | 4 oz | 1 cup |
| Salt | | | |
| Dried egg powder | 45 ml | 3 tbls | 3 tbls |
| Water | 90 ml | 6 tbls | 6 tbls |
| Milk | 275 ml | $\frac{1}{2}$ pt | $1\frac{1}{4}$ cups |
| Lard or dripping | 25 g | 1 oz | 2 tbls |
| Sausages | 450 g | 1 lb | 1 lb |

1. Sift the flour, salt and dried egg into a bowl. Make a well in the centre and add the water and half of the milk. Mix well and beat until smooth. Stir in the remaining milk.

2. Place the lard or dripping in a small roasting tin, heat in a hot oven at 220°C/425°F/Gas mark 7 for 3 minutes. Add the sausages and cook for 10 minutes. Pour in the batter, return to the oven and cook until risen and golden brown, about 30 minutes. Serve hot.

# Spicy Hamburgers

Makes 4

|  | Metric | Imperial | American |
|---|---|---|---|
| Lean minced beef | 350 g | 12 oz | $\frac{3}{4}$ lb |
| Grated onion | 15 ml | 1 tbls | 1 tbls |
| Fresh breadcrumbs | 30 ml | 2 tbls | 2 tbls |
| Ground cardamom | 5 ml | 1 tsp | 1 tsp |
| Salt and pepper | | | |
| Worcestershire sauce | 5 ml | 1 tsp | 1 tsp |
| Dried egg powder | 15 ml | 1 tbls | 1 tbls |
| Water | 15 ml | 1 tbls | 1 tbls |
| Oil for frying | | | |
| Hamburger buns | 4 | 4 | 4 |
| Sliced tomato | | | |
| Onion rings | | | |
| Gherkins | | | |

1. Mix together the minced beef, onion, breadcrumbs, cardamom, salt and pepper and Worcestershire sauce.

2. Blend the dried egg and water to a smooth paste and mix into the meat mixture. Turn on to a floured surface and form into 4 flat patties.

3. Heat the oil in large frying pan and fry the hamburgers for 3 minutes on each side for medium rare or 5 minutes on each side for well done.

4. Place each hamburger in a bun and top with sliced tomato, onion rings and a sliced gherkin. Serve with tomato ketchup and a side salad.

# Blanquette of Pork

Serves 4 to 6

|  | Metric | Imperial | American |
|---|---|---|---|
| Pie pork | 900 g | 2 lb | 2 lb |
| Water | 750 ml | $1\frac{1}{4}$ pt | 3 cups |
| Onions | 3 | 3 | 3 |
| Carrots | 2 | 2 | 2 |
| Bouquet garni | 1 | 1 | 1 |
| Salt and pepper | | | |
| Mushrooms | 100 g | 4 oz | $\frac{1}{4}$ lb |
| Butter | 50 g | 2 oz | $\frac{1}{4}$ cup |
| Lemon juice | 15 ml | 1 tbls | 1 tbls |
| Plain flour | 25 g | 1 oz | $\frac{1}{4}$ cup |
| Dried egg powder | 30 ml | 2 tbls | 2 tbls |
| Water | 30 ml | 2 tbls | 2 tbls |
| Single cream | 150 ml | $\frac{1}{4}$ pt | $\frac{2}{3}$ cup |
| Chopped parsley to garnish | | | |

1. Cut the pork into convenient-sized cubes. Place in a medium-sized saucepan with the water and bring to the boil. Skim.

2. Peel and quarter the onions. Scrape and slice the carrots. Add to the pork with the bouquet garni and seasoning. Bring back to the boil, cover and simmer gently until the pork is tender, about 1 hour.

3. Wipe and slice the mushrooms. Melt half the butter in a small saucepan. Add the mushrooms and lemon juice, cover and cook gently until the mushrooms are soft.

4. Melt the remaining butter in a pan, stir in the flour and cook for 1 minute. Strain the liquid from the cooked pork, discarding the bouquet garni. Gradually blend the liquid into the flour mixture and bring to the boil. Cook for 2 minutes.

5. Blend the dried egg and water to a smooth paste, then blend in the cream. Pour a little of the sauce on to the egg and cream mixture and stir well. Pour this into the sauce, stirring all the time. Add the pork, onions and carrots to the sauce, with the mushrooms and the liquid they were cooked in. Reheat, stirring, but do not allow to boil. Serve sprinkled with chopped parsley.

## Variation

**Blanquette of Veal:**  Replace the pork with stewing veal.

# Pork à la Crème

Serves 4

|  | Metric | Imperial | American |
|---|---|---|---|
| Pork tenderloin | 350 g | 12 oz | $\frac{3}{4}$ lb |
| Oil | 30 ml | 2 tbls | 2 tbls |
| Lemon juice | 15 ml | 1 tbls | 1 tbls |
| Large onion | 1 | 1 | 1 |
| Button mushrooms | 100 g | 4 oz | $\frac{1}{4}$ lb |
| Butter | 25 g | 1 oz | 2 tbls |
| Salt and pepper |  |  |  |
| Chicken stock | 150 ml | $\frac{1}{4}$ pt | $\frac{2}{3}$ cup |
| Dried egg powder | 30 ml | 2 tbls | 2 tbls |
| Water | 30 ml | 2 tbls | 2 tbls |
| Single cream | 150 ml | $\frac{1}{4}$ pt | $\frac{2}{3}$ cup |
| Chopped parsley | 15 ml | 1 tbls | 1 tbls |

**1.** Trim any fat from the pork tenderloin. Cut the meat across the grain into 1 cm/$\frac{1}{2}$ in slices. Place in a bowl and add 15 ml/1 tbls each of oil and lemon juice. Mix well and leave to marinate for 30 minutes.

**2.** Peel and slice the onion. Clean and slice the mushrooms. Heat the remaining oil and the butter in a frying pan. Drain the pork from the marinade and fry the slices quickly on each side until lightly browned. Remove from the pan. Add the onion and mushrooms to the pan and fry until soft. Season with salt and pepper.

**3.** Add the chicken stock to the pan and cook quickly until reduced by about a third. Blend the egg powder and water to a smooth paste, then blend in the cream. Reduce the heat under the frying pan, add the cream mixture and stir until well mixed.

**4.** Return the pork to the pan and reheat very gently. Do not allow to boil. Sprinkle with chopped parsley and serve with mashed potatoes and a green vegetable.

# Leicester Cheese Pudding

Serves 4

|  | Metric | Imperial | American |
|---|---|---|---|
| Milk | 275 ml | $\frac{1}{2}$ pt | $1\frac{1}{4}$ cups |
| Fresh white breadcrumbs | 75 g | 3 oz | $1\frac{1}{2}$ cups |
| Butter or margarine | 50 g | 2 oz | $\frac{1}{4}$ cup |
| Dried egg powder | 30 ml | 2 tbls | 2 tbls |
| Water | 30 ml | 2 tbls | 2 tbls |
| Leicester cheese, grated | 100 g | 4 oz | 1 cup |
| Grated onion | 15 ml | 1 tbls | 1 tbls |
| Salt and pepper |  |  |  |
| Dried egg white | 15 ml | 1 tbls | 1 tbls |
| Water | 60 ml | 4 tbls | 4 tbls |

1. Heat the milk to boiling point, pour on to the breadcrumbs and mix well. Stir in the butter or margarine.

2. Blend the dried egg and the 30 ml/2 tbls of water to a smooth paste, then stir it into the breadcrumbs with the cheese and onion. Season with salt and pepper.

3. Blend the egg white with 15 ml/1 tbls of water until smooth. Blend in the remaining water. Whisk until stiff. Fold into the breadcrumb mixture.

4. Grease a 1 litre/$1\frac{3}{4}$ pt/$4\frac{1}{2}$ cup pie dish. Pour in the pudding mixture and bake in the centre of a moderately hot oven at 190°C/375°F/Gas mark 5 for 25 to 30 minutes. Serve immediately with tomato sauce.

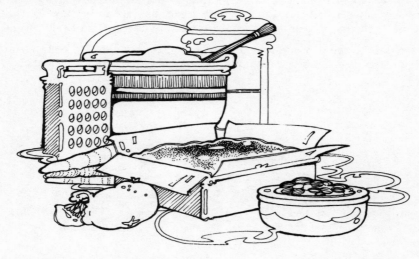

# Spinach and Mushroom Roulade

Serves 4

|  | Metric | Imperial | American |
|---|---|---|---|
| **Roulade** | | | |
| Fresh spinach | 450 g | 1 lb | 1 lb |
| Butter | 15 g | $\frac{1}{2}$ oz | 1 tbls |
| Salt and pepper | | | |
| Grated nutmeg | | | |
| Dried egg powder | 60 ml | 4 tbls | 4 tbls |
| Water | 60 ml | 4 tbls | 4 tbls |
| Dried egg white | 30 ml | 2 tbls | 2 tbls |
| Water | 120 ml | 8 tbls | 8 tbls |
| Grated Parmesan cheese | 15 ml | 1 tbls | 1 tbls |
| **Filling** | | | |
| Mushrooms | 100 g | 4 oz | $\frac{1}{4}$ lb |
| Butter | 25 g | 1 oz | 2 tbls |
| Plain flour | 15 ml | 1 tbls | 1 tbls |
| Single cream | 150 ml | $\frac{1}{4}$ pt | $\frac{2}{3}$ cup |
| Lemon juice | 5 ml | 1 tsp | 1 tsp |

1. Grease a 30 × 20 mm/12 × 8 in Swiss roll tin and line with baking parchment. Lightly grease the parchment.

2. Remove the stalks and wash the spinach well. Shake dry and place in a saucepan without water. Cover with a lid and cook until tender. Drain well, pressing out all the moisture. Chop, then add the butter and season with salt, pepper and a pinch of nutmeg.

3. Blend the dried egg with the 60 ml/4 tbls of water and mix into the spinach.

4. Blend the egg white with 30 ml/2 tbls of water until smooth, then stir in the remaining water. Whisk until stiff. Fold into the spinach with a metal spoon. Spread into the prepared tin and cook in a moderately hot oven at 200°C/400°F/Gas mark 6 for about 15 minutes. The mixture should spring back when pressed lightly with a finger.

5. To make the filling: Wipe and chop the mushrooms. Melt the butter, add the mushrooms and fry gently until just tender. Stir in the flour and cook for 1 minute. Add the cream and lemon juice and bring to the boil. Simmer for 1 minute. Keep the filling hot.

6. Sprinkle a sheet of greaseproof paper with the Parmesan. Invert the spinach mixture on to the paper, spread with the hot filling and roll up, using the paper to help. Slide on to a warm serving dish and serve warm, cut into slices.

# Cheese Soufflé

Serves 3 to 4

|  | Metric | Imperial | American |
|---|---|---|---|
| Butter | 50 g | 2 oz | $\frac{1}{4}$ cup |
| Plain flour | 50 g | 2 oz | $\frac{1}{2}$ cup |
| Milk | 275 ml | $\frac{1}{2}$ pt | $1\frac{1}{4}$ cups |
| Cayenne pepper |  |  |  |
| Salt |  |  |  |
| Dry mustard powder | 5 ml | 1 tsp | 1 tsp |
| Dried egg powder | 45 ml | 3 tbls | 3 tbls |
| Water | 45 ml | 3 tbls | 3 tbls |
| Cheddar cheese, grated | 100 g | 4 oz | 1 cup |
| Dried egg white | 30 ml | 2 tbls | 2 tbls |
| Water | 120 ml | 8 tbls | 8 tbls |

1. Butter a 1·15 litre/2 pt/5 cup soufflé dish.

2. Melt the butter in a saucepan, stir in the flour and cook for 2 minutes. Remove from the heat and blend in the milk, return to the heat and bring to the boil, stirring. Cook for 3 minutes, stirring continuously. Add a pinch of cayenne pepper, salt and the mustard.

3. Blend the dried egg with the 45 ml/3 tbls of water to a smooth paste, add to the sauce with the cheese and mix well.

4. Blend the dried egg white with 30 ml/2 tbls of the water until smooth. Blend in the remaining water and whisk until very stiff. Fold a spoonful into the cheese sauce, then fold the cheese mixture into the whisked egg white, lightly but thoroughly.

5. Turn into the prepared soufflé dish and cook in the centre of a moderately hot oven at 190°C/375°F/Gas mark 5 for 35 to 40 minutes until well risen and golden brown. The soufflé should be firm on the outside but fairly soft inside. Serve at once.

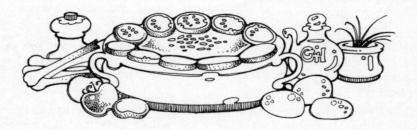

# Leek and Bacon Flan

Serves 4

|  | Metric | Imperial | American |
|---|---|---|---|
| **Cheese pastry** | | | |
| Soft margarine | 100 g | 4 oz | $\frac{1}{2}$ cup |
| Water | 20 ml | 4 tsp | 4 tsp |
| Plain flour | 175 g | 6 oz | $1\frac{1}{2}$ cups |
| Cheddar cheese, grated | 75 g | 3 oz | $\frac{3}{4}$ cup |
| Salt | | | |
| Cayenne pepper | | | |
| Dry mustard | | | |
| **Filling** | | | |
| Leeks | 450 g | 1 lb | 1 lb |
| Streaky bacon | 100 g | 4 oz | $\frac{1}{4}$ lb |
| Butter or margarine | 25 g | 1 oz | 2 tbls |
| Milk | 150 ml | $\frac{1}{4}$ pt | $\frac{2}{3}$ cup |
| Single cream | 150 ml | $\frac{1}{4}$ pt | $\frac{2}{3}$ cup |
| Dried egg powder | 60 ml | 4 tbls | 4 tbls |
| Water | 60 ml | 4 tbls | 4 tbls |
| Salt and pepper | | | |
| Cheddar cheese, grated | 25 g | 1 oz | $\frac{1}{4}$ cup |
| Fresh breadcrumbs | 45 ml | 3 tbls | 3 tbls |

1. Place the margarine, water and 3 rounded tablespoons of the flour in a bowl and cream with a fork until well mixed. Add the remaining flour, the cheese, a pinch of salt, cayenne and mustard powder and work together to form a firm dough. Knead lightly until smooth. Place in a polythene bag and chill for 30 minutes. Roll out on a floured surface and line 20 cm/8 in flan ring on a baking sheet.

2. Line the flan with a circle of greaseproof paper, weigh down with dried beans and bake the flan just above the centre of a moderately hot oven at 200°C/400°F/Gas mark 6 for 15 minutes. Carefully lift out the paper and beans and return the flan to the oven for 5 minutes to dry out the centre.

3. Wash, trim and slice the leeks and rinse the slices under running water to make sure all the grit is removed. De-rind the bacon and cut it into strips.

4. Melt the butter or margarine in a saucepan, add the leeks and bacon and fry until the leeks are tender, about 10 minutes. Remove from the heat.

5. Mix the milk and cream together. Blend the dried egg and water to a smooth cream, then stir in the milk mixture. Stir into the leeks and bacon, season with salt and pepper and turn into the flan case. Mix the cheese and breadcrumbs and sprinkle over the filling. Bake in a moderately hot oven at 190°C/375°F/Gas mark 5 until the filling is set and the topping crisp and golden, about 30 minutes. Serve warm.

# Cheese and Spinach Rissoles

Serves 3

|  | Metric | Imperial | American |
|---|---|---|---|
| *Frozen chopped spinach* | *225 g* | *8 oz* | $\frac{1}{2}$ *lb* |
| *Butter* | *25 g* | *1 oz* | *2 tbls* |
| *Fresh breadcrumbs* | *25 g* | *1 oz* | $\frac{1}{3}$ *cup* |
| *Cheddar cheese, grated* | *75 g* | *3 oz* | $\frac{3}{4}$ *cup* |
| *Grated nutmeg* | | | |
| *Salt and pepper* | | | |
| *Dried egg powder* | *45 ml* | *3 tbls* | *3 tbls* |
| *Water* | *60 ml* | *4 tbls* | *4 tbls* |
| *Dried breadcrumbs* | *50 g* | *2 oz* | $\frac{1}{2}$ *cup* |
| *Oil for frying* | | | |

1. Place the spinach in a saucepan and heat gently until thawed, stirring occasionally. Bring to the boil, reduce the heat and cook gently for about 4 minutes until fairly dry. Place in a sieve and press out all the moisture.

2. Turn the spinach into a bowl and add the butter, breadcrumbs and cheese. Add a pinch of nutmeg and season well with salt and pepper.

3. Blend the dried egg and water to a smooth cream. Add half to the spinach mixture and mix well. Chill for 1 hour.

4. Turn the spinach mixture on to a floured surface and shape into 6 rissoles. Dip each rissole into the reserved egg and then in dried breadcrumbs.

5. Heat about 5 mm/$\frac{1}{4}$ in of oil in a large frying pan and fry the rissoles until golden brown on all sides. Serve hot with mashed potato.

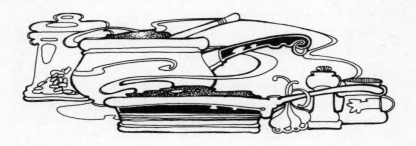

# Bacon and Egg Flan

Serves 4 to 6

|  | Metric | Imperial | American |
|---|---|---|---|
| **Pastry** | | | |
| Plain flour | 175 g | 6 oz | 1½ cups |
| Margarine or butter | 40 g | 1½ oz | 3 tbls |
| Lard or vegetable fat | 40 g | 1½ oz | 3 tbls |
| Water | 30 ml | 2 tbls | 2 tbls |
| **Filling** | | | |
| Small onion | 1 | 1 | 1 |
| Streaky bacon | 100 g | 4 oz | ¼ lb |
| Oil | 15 ml | 1 tbls | 1 tbls |
| Cheddar cheese, grated | 100 g | 4 oz | ¼ lb |
| Dried egg powder | 45 ml | 3 tbls | 3 tbls |
| Water | 45 ml | 3 tbls | 3 tbls |
| Milk | 150 ml | ¼ pt | ⅔ cup |
| Single cream | 150 ml | ¼ pt | ⅔ cup |
| Salt and pepper | | | |

1. Sift the flour into a bowl, add the fats, cut into small pieces, and rub in with the fingertips until the mixture resembles fine breadcrumbs. Add about 30 ml/2 tbls of water and mix to form a firm dough. Roll out on a floured surface and use to line a 20 cm/8 in flan ring on a baking sheet.

2. Peel and thinly slice the onion. De-rind the bacon and cut it into small pieces. Fry the bacon and onion in the oil until lightly browned. Cool, then spread in the flan. Sprinkle the cheese over the top.

3. Mix the dried egg to a smooth cream with the water. Blend in the milk, then the cream. Season with salt and pepper. Pour into the flan.

4. Cook the flan in the centre of a moderately hot oven at 200°C/400°F/Gas mark 6 for 15 minutes. Reduce the temperature to 180°C/350°F/Gas mark 4 and cook for a further 15 to 20 minutes or until the flan is golden brown. Serve warm or cold.

# Fresh Herb Pasta

Serves 3 to 4

|  | Metric | Imperial | American |
|---|---|---|---|
| *Plain flour* | *350 g* | *12 oz* | *3 cups* |
| *Salt* |  |  |  |
| *Dried egg powder* | *60 ml* | *4 tbls* | *4 tbls* |
| *Chopped, fresh mixed herbs* | *60 ml* | *4 tbls* | *4 tbls* |
| *Water* | *175 ml* | *6 fl oz* | *$\frac{3}{4}$ cup* |
| *Olive oil* |  |  |  |
| *Parmesan cheese to serve* |  |  |  |

1. Sift the flour, a pinch of salt and the dried egg into a bowl. Add the herbs and water and mix to a dough.

2. Turn the dough on to a lightly floured surface and knead until smooth, 10 to 15 minutes. Wrap in cling film and leave to rest for 30 minutes.

3. Cut the dough in half and roll out one half to a rectangle 45 × 30 cm/18 × 12 in. Cut into 5 mm/$\frac{1}{4}$ in wide strips. Hang the strips on a clean tea towel over the back of a chair while rolling and cutting the remaining dough.

4. Bring a large saucepan of salted water to the boil. Add the pasta and bring back to the boil. Cook until just tender, about 3 minutes. Drain and toss in a little olive oil. Serve sprinkled generously with Parmesan cheese.

# VEGETABLE DISHES

Really fresh vegetables are probably nicest when simply cooked, possibly tossed with a knob of butter or with a well-flavoured sauce. However, there are some delicious recipes which have egg added and they are included in this chapter.

# Duchesse Potatoes

Serves 2 to 3

|  | Metric | Imperial | American |
|---|---|---|---|
| Old potatoes | 450 g | 1 lb | 1 lb |
| Dried egg powder | 45 ml | 3 tbls | 3 tbls |
| Water | 75 ml | 5 tbls | 5 tbls |
| Milk | 15 ml | 1 tbls | 1 tbls |
| Butter | 25 g | 1 oz | 2 tbls |
| Salt and pepper | | | |
| Grated nutmeg | | | |
| Chopped parsley or paprika to serve | | | |

1. Peel the potatoes and cut into even-sized pieces. Place in a saucepan of cold salted water. Bring to the boil and cook until tender. Sieve, put through a vegetable mill or mash very smoothly.

2. Mix the dried egg with the water and milk to a smooth cream. Reserve about 2 tablespoons of the mixture. Mix the remainder into the potatoes with the butter. Season well with salt, pepper and nutmeg.

3. Place the potato in a piping bag fitted with a large star tube and pipe cone shapes on to a greased baking sheet. Cook in a moderately hot oven at 200°C/400°F/Gas mark 6 for 5 minutes.

4. Brush with the reserved egg and return to the oven until golden brown, about 10 minutes more. Serve hot, sprinkled with chopped parsley or paprika. Alternatively, to make a border for a starter or main dish, pipe the potato around edge of a flameproof dish, brush with the reserved egg and brown under a moderate grill.

# Cheesy Potato Balls

Serves 4

|  | Metric | Imperial | American |
|---|---|---|---|
| Potatoes | 450 g | 1 lb | 1 lb |
| Dried egg powder | 60 ml | 4 tbls | 4 tbls |
| Water | 120 ml | 8 tbls | 8 tbls |
| Cheddar cheese, grated | 75 g | 3 oz | $\frac{3}{4}$ cup |
| Salt and pepper |  |  |  |
| Plain flour | 25 g | 1 oz | $\frac{1}{4}$ cup |
| Fresh white breadcrumbs | 50 g | 2 oz | 1 cup |
| Oil for deep frying |  |  |  |

1. Peel the potatoes and then cut into pieces. Place in a saucepan, cover with salted water, bring to the boil and cook until tender. Drain well, then mash thoroughly.

2. Mix the dried egg and water to a smooth cream and reserve 4 tablespoons of the egg. Beat the remainder into the potato with the cheese and seasoning. Leave to cool.

3. Form the potato mixture into balls about the size of a large walnut, then roll them in the flour. Dip the balls in the reserved egg then roll in the breadcrumbs to coat.

4. Heat the oil to 190°C/375°F. Place the potato balls, a few at a time, in a frying basket and fry in deep fat until golden. Drain on kitchen paper, serve hot with grills, steak or lamb chops.

# Potato Gnocchi

Serves 4

|  | Metric | Imperial | American |
|---|---|---|---|
| Potatoes | 450 g | 1 lb | 1 lb |
| Salt and pepper | | | |
| Grated nutmeg | 2.5 ml | $\frac{1}{2}$ tsp | $\frac{1}{2}$ tsp |
| Plain flour | 150 g | 4 oz | 1 cup |
| Dried egg powder | 30 ml | 2 tbls | 2 tbls |
| Water | 45 ml | 3 tbls | 3 tbls |
| Butter | 50 g | 2 oz | $\frac{1}{4}$ cup |
| Grated Parmesan cheese | 50 g | 2 oz | $\frac{1}{2}$ cup |

1. Peel the potatoes and cut into small chunks. Put in a saucepan, cover with salted water and bring to the boil. Cook for 15 to 20 minutes or until tender. Drain and mash very smoothly.

2. Season the potatoes to taste with salt and pepper. Beat in the nutmeg and flour.

3. Mix the dried egg and water to a smooth cream and mix into the potatoes. Turn on to a lightly floured work surface and knead lightly. Form into a roll and cut into 24 equal pieces. Knead each piece into a ball.

4. Bring a large saucepan of salted water to the boil. Drop the potato balls, about 8 at a time, into the water and simmer for about 5 minutes or until the balls rise to the surface. Remove with a draining spoon and place in a buttered dish. Keep hot. Cook the remaining balls in the same way.

5. Melt the butter and pour over the gnocchi, sprinkle with Parmesan cheese and serve hot.

# Spinach Gnocchi

Serves 4

|  | Metric | Imperial | American |
|---|---|---|---|
| *Frozen chopped spinach* | *450 g* | *1 lb* | *1 lb* |
| *Butter* | *50 g* | *2 oz* | *$\frac{1}{4}$ cup* |
| *Curd cheese* | *225 g* | *8 oz* | *1 cup* |
| *Dried egg powder* | *60 ml* | *4 tbls* | *4 tbls* |
| *Water* | *60 ml* | *4 tbls* | *4 tbls* |
| *Single cream* | *30 ml* | *2 tbls* | *2 tbls* |
| *Plain flour* | *50 g* | *2 oz* | *$\frac{1}{2}$ cup* |
| *Grated Parmesan cheese* | *50 g* | *2 oz* | *$\frac{1}{2}$ cup* |
| *Salt and pepper* | | | |
| *Grated nutmeg* | *2.5 ml* | *$\frac{1}{2}$ tsp* | *$\frac{1}{2}$ tsp* |
| *Tomato sauce to serve* | | | |

1. Place the spinach in a saucepan and cook over a low heat without additional water until thawed. Stir over the heat until dry. Place in a sieve and press out any moisture. Return to the pan and add the butter and curd cheese. Beat until smooth.

2. Mix the dried egg and water to a smooth cream and beat into the spinach mixture. Stir in the cream, flour, Parmesan, seasoning to taste and nutmeg. Turn the mixture into a shallow dish and leave to cool. Chill for 1 hour.

3. Bring a large saucepan of salted water to the boil. Shape the spinach mixture into balls about the size of a small walnut and drop into the simmering water, about 8 at a time. Cook until the gnocchi rise to the surface, about 3 minutes. Remove with a draining spoon and place in a warm, buttered dish. Keep hot. Cook the remaining gnocchi in the same way.

4. Serve the gnocchi with a well-flavoured tomato sauce and extra Parmesan.

# Souffléd Sprouts

Serves 4

|  | Metric | Imperial | American |
|---|---|---|---|
| Brussels sprouts | 450 g | 1 lb | 1 lb |
| Single cream | 150 ml | $\frac{1}{4}$ pt | $\frac{2}{3}$ cup |
| Potatoes | 350 g | 12 oz | $\frac{3}{4}$ lb |
| Butter | 25 g | 1 oz | 2 tbls |
| Salt and pepper |  |  |  |
| Grated nutmeg |  |  |  |
| Dried egg white | 30 ml | 2 tbls | 2 tbls |
| Water | 120 ml | 8 tbls | 8 tbls |

1. Trim and wash the sprouts. Cook in boiling salted water for 5 minutes. Drain and purée in a blender or food processor with the cream.

2. Peel and cut up the potatoes. Cook in boiling salted water until tender. Drain and mash until smooth. Stir in the sprout purée and butter and mix well. Season with salt, pepper and a pinch of nutmeg.

3. Blend the dried egg white and 30 ml/2 tbls of the water until smooth, then blend in the remaining water. Whisk until stiff. Fold into the sprout mixture.

4. Turn the mixture into a lightly greased 1 litre/$1\frac{3}{4}$ pt/$4\frac{1}{4}$ cup soufflé dish and cook in the centre of a moderately hot oven at 190°C/375°F/Gas mark 5 until risen and golden brown, about 40 minutes.

# Parsnip Bake

Serves 4

|  | Metric | Imperial | American |
|---|---|---|---|
| Parsnips | 675 g | $1\frac{1}{2}$ lb | $1\frac{1}{2}$ lb |
| Butter or margarine | 50 g | 2 oz | $\frac{1}{4}$ cup |
| Plain flour | 50 g | 2 oz | $\frac{1}{2}$ cup |
| Milk | 275 ml | $\frac{1}{2}$ pt | $1\frac{1}{4}$ cups |
| Salt and pepper |  |  |  |
| Caraway seeds | 5 ml | 1 tsp | 1 tsp |
| Dried egg powder | 60 ml | 4 tbls | 4 tbls |
| Water | 120 ml | 8 tbls | 8 tbls |
| Dried breadcrumbs | 30 ml | 2 tbls | 2 tbls |
| Cheddar cheese, grated | 25 g | 1 oz | $\frac{1}{4}$ cup |

1. Peel and cut up the parsnips, place in a saucepan, cover with salted water and bring to the boil. Cover and cook until tender, about 20 minutes. Drain and mash well.

2. Melt the butter or margarine in a saucepan, add the flour and cook, stirring, for 2 minutes. Remove from the heat and blend in the milk. Bring to the boil, stirring, and cook for 2 minutes. Season with salt and pepper and add the caraway seeds and mashed parsnips.

3. Blend the dried egg and water to a smooth cream, then stir into the parsnip mixture. Turn into a greased 1.75 litre/3 pt/$7\frac{1}{2}$ cup ovenproof dish. Mix the breadcrumbs and cheese together and sprinkle over the parsnips.

4. Bake in the centre of a moderately hot oven at 200°C/400°F/Gas mark 6 for 30 minutes or until the topping is brown and the parsnip mixture has heated through. Serve hot with cold meats or mince.

# Pease Pudding

Serves 4

|  | Metric | Imperial | American |
|---|---|---|---|
| Dried split peas | 225 g | 8 oz | $\frac{1}{2}$ lb |
| Onion | 1 | 1 | 1 |
| Butter or margarine | 25 g | 1 oz | 2 tbls |
| Dried egg powder | 30 ml | 2 tbls | 2 tbls |
| Water | 60 ml | 4 tbls | 4 tbls |
| Caster sugar | | | |
| Salt and pepper | | | |
| Chopped parsley | 15 ml | 1 tbls | 1 tbls |

1. Soak the peas in cold water for several hours or overnight. Drain, place in a saucepan, cover with fresh water and bring to the boil. Peel and slice the onion, add to the peas, cover the pan and simmer until the peas are tender, about $1\frac{1}{2}$ hours. Drain.

2. Place the peas and onion in a blender or food processor with the butter or margarine. Blend the dried egg and water to a smooth cream and add to the peas with a pinch of sugar and seasoning. Process until smooth. Turn into a dish and sprinkle with parsley. Serve with boiled ham, bacon or pickled pork.

# Corn Fritters

Makes 8

|  | Metric | Imperial | American |
|---|---|---|---|
| Self-raising flour | 100 g | 4 oz | 1 cup |
| Salt | 2.5 ml | $\frac{1}{2}$ tsp | $\frac{1}{2}$ tsp |
| Dry mustard powder | 2.5 ml | $\frac{1}{2}$ tsp | $\frac{1}{2}$ tsp |
| Dried egg powder | 30 ml | 2 tbls | 2 tbls |
| Milk | 150 ml | $\frac{1}{4}$ pt | $\frac{2}{3}$ cup |
| Dried egg white | 15 ml | 1 tbls | 1 tbls |
| Water | 60 ml | 4 tbls | 4 tbls |
| Can of sweetcorn niblets (350 g/12 oz) | 1 | 1 | 1 |
| Oil for frying | | | |

1. Sift the flour, salt, mustard and dried egg into a bowl. Gradually blend in the milk to make a smooth batter.

2. Blend the egg white and 15 ml/1 tbls of water until smooth. Stir in the remaining water. Whisk until stiff.

3. Fold the contents of the can of sweetcorn into the batter, then fold in the whisked egg white.

4. Heat about 5 mm/$\frac{1}{4}$ in of oil in a frying pan. Drop spoonsful of the fritter mixture into the hot oil and cook until golden underneath. Turn and cook on the other side. Fry the remaining fritters in the same way. Serve hot with grilled bacon and tomatoes.

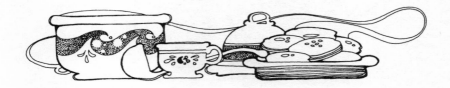

# SAUCES

Many sauces have raw or partially cooked egg as the essential ingredient. But by using dried or frozen pasteurised eggs such great classic sauces as Hollandaise, Bernaise and Aioli can still be enjoyed, as can a superb Egg Custard Sauce which is essential for a realy authentic trifle.

# Mayonnaise

Makes about 275 ml/$\frac{1}{2}$ pt/1$\frac{1}{4}$ cups

|  | Metric | Imperial | American |
|---|---|---|---|
| Dried egg powder | 30 ml | 2 tbls | 2 tbls |
| Lemon juice | 45 ml | 3 tbls | 3 tbls |
| Dijon mustard | 10 ml | 2 tsp | 2 tsp |
| Salt | 2.5 ml | $\frac{1}{2}$ tsp | $\frac{1}{2}$ tsp |
| Pepper | 2.5 ml | $\frac{1}{2}$ tsp | $\frac{1}{2}$ tsp |
| Caster sugar | 2.5 ml | $\frac{1}{2}$ tsp | $\frac{1}{2}$ tsp |
| Corn or olive oil | 225 ml | 8 fl oz | 1 cup |

1. Place the egg powder, 30 ml/2 tbls of lemon juice, the mustard, salt, pepper and sugar in a basin. Whisk until smooth.

2. While whisking, add the oil a spoonful at a time to start with, whisking well after each addition. Once half the oil has been added, whisk in the remaining lemon juice. Then add the remaining oil in a very thin stream, whisking all the time until the mayonnaise has reached the desired consistency.

3. If the mayonnaise becomes too thick before all the oil has been added, thin with a tablespoon of boiling water or extra lemon juice. Store in a covered jar in the refrigerator for up to a week.

**Note**
Wrap a tea towel around base of the basin with the ends hanging over the edge of the work surface and lean on these ends to secure the basin while using one hand to whisk and the other to pour in the oil.

**Variation**

*Aïoli:* Crush 2 to 3 cloves of garlic to a smooth paste and add to the egg mixture, then add the oil as above. Serve with raw vegetables as a dip or add to fish soups.

# Blender Mayonnaise

Makes about 275 ml/$\frac{1}{2}$ pt/$1\frac{1}{4}$ cups

|  | Metric | Imperial | American |
|---|---|---|---|
| *Frozen pasteurised egg, thawed* | *60 ml* | *4 tbls* | *4 tbls* |
| *Vinegar* | *30 ml* | *2 tbls* | *2 tbls* |
| *Dry mustard powder* | *5 ml* | *1 tsp* | *1 tsp* |
| *Caster sugar* | *5 ml* | *1 tsp* | *1 tsp* |
| *Salt* | *2.5 ml* | *$\frac{1}{2}$ tsp* | *$\frac{1}{2}$ tsp* |
| *White pepper* | *2.5 ml* | *$\frac{1}{2}$ tsp* | *$\frac{1}{2}$ tsp* |
| *Corn oil* | *275 ml* | *$\frac{1}{2}$ pt* | *$1\frac{1}{4}$ cups* |

**1.** Place the egg, vinegar, mustard, sugar, salt and pepper in a liquidiser or food processor bowl and run the machine for a few seconds until they form a smooth paste. Scrape down from the sides.

**2.** Run the machine again and pour the oil through the hole in lid of the blender or funnel of the processor in a thin steady stream. The mayonnaise will become thick and creamy. If it is too thick, add 15–30 ml/1–2 tbls of boiling water or more vinegar to achieve the desired consistency.

# Tartare Sauce

Makes about 275 ml/$\frac{1}{2}$ pt/$1\frac{1}{4}$ cups

|  | Metric | Imperial | American |
| --- | --- | --- | --- |
| Dried egg powder | 30 ml | 2 tbls | 2 tbls |
| Lemon juice | 45 ml | 3 tbls | 3 tbls |
| Salt and pepper |  |  |  |
| Dry mustard | 2.5 ml | $\frac{1}{2}$ tsp | $\frac{1}{2}$ tsp |
| Caster sugar | 2.5 ml | $\frac{1}{2}$ tsp | $\frac{1}{2}$ tsp |
| Corn oil | 275 ml | $\frac{1}{2}$ pt | $1\frac{1}{4}$ cups |
| Gherkins | 3 | 3 | 3 |
| Stuffed green olives | 4 | 4 | 4 |
| Pickled onions | 2 | 2 | 2 |
| Chopped parsley | 15 ml | 1 tbls | 1 tbls |
| Capers | 15 ml | 1 tbls | 1 tbls |

1. Place the dried egg, 30 ml/2 tbls of the lemon juice, a pinch of salt and pepper, the mustard and sugar in a basin and whisk until smooth.

2. Gradually whisk in the oil, a spoonful at a time at first, then more quickly. After half the oil has been added, whisk in the remaining lemon juice, then continue adding the oil.

3. Chop the gherkins, olives and pickled onions. Add to the sauce with the parsley and capers and mix well.

4. Turn into a dish and serve the sauce with grilled or fried fish dishes.

# Hot Tartare Sauce

Makes about 275 ml/$\frac{1}{2}$ pt/1$\frac{1}{4}$ cups

|  | Metric | Imperial | American |
|---|---|---|---|
| Butter | 25 g | 1 oz | 2 tbls |
| Plain flour | 25 g | 1 oz | $\frac{1}{4}$ cup |
| Milk | 275 ml | $\frac{1}{2}$ pt | 1$\frac{1}{4}$ cups |
| Salt and pepper |  |  |  |
| Dried egg powder | 15 ml | 1 tbls | 1 tbls |
| Lemon juice | 30 ml | 2 tbls | 2 tbls |
| Chopped parsley | 15 ml | 1 tbls | 1 tbls |
| Chopped gherkin | 15 ml | 1 tbls | 1 tbls |
| Chopped capers | 15 ml | 1 tbls | 1 tbls |

1. Melt the butter in a small saucepan, add the flour and cook for 2 minutes. Blend in the milk, bring to the boil and cook for 3 minutes. Season with salt and pepper.

2. Blend the dried egg and lemon juice to a smooth paste, then stir it into the sauce with the remaining ingredients. Reheat, but do not boil. Serve hot with fried or grilled fish.

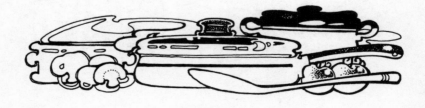

# Hollandaise Sauce

Makes about 150 ml/$\frac{1}{4}$ pt/$\frac{2}{3}$ cup

|  | Metric | Imperial | American |
| --- | --- | --- | --- |
| Dried egg powder | 30 ml | 2 tbls | 2 tbls |
| Water | 15 ml | 1 tbls | 1 tbls |
| Lemon juice | 30 ml | 2 tbls | 2 tbls |
| Salt and pepper | | | |
| Softened butter | 100 g | 4 oz | $\frac{1}{2}$ cup |

1. Blend the dried egg, water and lemon juice to a smooth paste in a basin. Season with salt and pepper.

2. Place the basin over a pan of gently simmering water and whisk the egg until it starts to thicken.

3. Add the butter a small piece at a time, whisking continuously, until all the butter has been added and the sauce is the consistency of mayonnaise. Serve the sauce warm. It may be kept warm for a short time over the pan of warm water.

# Blender Hollandaise Sauce

Makes about 150 ml/$\frac{1}{4}$ pt/$\frac{2}{3}$ cup

|  | Metric | Imperial | American |
|---|---|---|---|
| *Frozen pasteurised egg, thawed* | *50 ml* | *2 fl oz* | *$\frac{1}{4}$ cup* |
| *Lemon juice* | *15 ml* | *1 tbls* | *1 tbls* |
| *Salt and pepper* | | | |
| *Butter* | *100 g* | *4 oz* | *$\frac{1}{2}$ cup* |

**1.** Put the egg, lemon juice and a little salt and pepper in a blender goblet. Run the machine until the ingredients are well mixed.

**2.** Heat the butter in a small saucepan until the sizzling stops, but do not allow to brown.

**3.** Run the blender, and pour the butter slowly on to the egg mixture through the hole in the lid. The sauce will thicken and become the texture of mayonnaise. Turn at once into a small bowl and serve warm.

# Mock Hollandaise Sauce

Makes about 275 ml/$\frac{1}{2}$ pt/1$\frac{1}{4}$ cups

|  | Metric | Imperial | American |
|---|---|---|---|
| Butter | 25 g | 1 oz | 2 tbls |
| Plain flour | 25 g | 1 oz | $\frac{1}{4}$ cup |
| Milk | 275 ml | $\frac{1}{2}$ pt | 1$\frac{1}{4}$ cups |
| Dried egg powder | 30 ml | 2 tbls | 2 tbls |
| Lemon juice | 45 ml | 3 tbls | 3 tbls |
| Cayenne pepper |  |  |  |
| Salt |  |  |  |

1. Melt the butter in a small saucepan, add the flour and cook for 2 minutes. Gradually blend in the milk and bring to the boil. Cook for 3 minutes.

2. Blend the dried egg and lemon juice to a smooth cream. Stir into the sauce and season with cayenne and salt. Reheat without boiling. Serve with grilled, steamed or fried fish or vegetables.

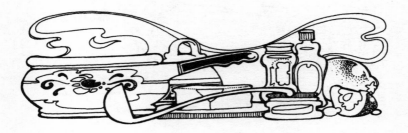

# Bearnaise Sauce

Makes about 150 ml/$\frac{1}{4}$ pt/$\frac{2}{3}$ cup

|  | Metric | Imperial | American |
|---|---|---|---|
| *Peppercorns* | *6* | *6* | *6* |
| *Small onion, chopped* | *1* | *1* | *1* |
| *Tarragon vinegar* | *30 ml* | *2 tbls* | *2 tbls* |
| *Water* | *45 ml* | *3 tbls* | *3 tbls* |
| *Dried egg powder* | *30 ml* | *2 tbls* | *2 tbls* |
| *Softened butter* | *100 g* | *4 oz* | *$\frac{1}{2}$ cup* |

**1.** Put the peppercorns, onion, vinegar and 15 ml/1 tbls of water in a small saucepan. Bring to the boil and cook until reduced by half.

**2.** Blend the remaining water and dried egg to a smooth paste in a basin. Strain on the reduced liquor and place the basin over a pan of simmering water. Whisk until the mixture begins to thicken.

**3.** Add the butter, a small piece at a time, whisking continuously until all the butter has been added. The sauce should be the consistency of mayonnaise. Serve warm with grilled or fried meat. The sauce may be kept warm for a short time over hot water, but cannot be reheated.

# Allemande Sauce

Makes about 275 ml/$\frac{1}{2}$ pt/$1\frac{1}{4}$ cups

|  | Metric | Imperial | American |
|---|---|---|---|
| Butter | 25 g | 1 oz | 2 tbls |
| Plain flour | 25 g | 1 oz | $\frac{1}{4}$ cup |
| Chicken stock | 275 ml | $\frac{1}{2}$ pt | $1\frac{1}{4}$ cups |
| Dried egg powder | 30 ml | 2 tbls | 2 tbls |
| Water | 30 ml | 2 tbls | 2 tbls |
| Single cream | 30 ml | 2 tbls | 2 tbls |
| Lemon juice | 10 ml | 2 tsp | 2 tsp |
| Salt and pepper |  |  |  |

1. Melt the butter in a small saucepan, stir in the flour and cook for 2 minutes. Gradually blend in the stock and bring to the boil. Cook, stirring, for 3 minutes.

2. Blend the dried egg and water to a smooth paste, blend in the cream and lemon juice. Remove the sauce from the heat and stir in the egg mixture. Season to taste with salt and pepper. Reheat the sauce without boiling. Serve hot with chicken and vegetable dishes.

# Sabayon Sauce

Makes about 150 ml/$\frac{1}{4}$ pt/$\frac{2}{3}$ cup

|  | Metric | Imperial | American |
|---|---|---|---|
| *Frozen pasteurised egg, thawed* | *90 ml* | *6 tbls* | *6 tbls* |
| *Sweet sherry* | *30 ml* | *2 tbls* | *2 tbls* |
| *Icing sugar* | *30 ml* | *2 tbls* | *2 tbls* |

1. Place the egg in a basin, blend in the sherry, stir in the icing sugar.

2. Place the basin over a pan of simmering water and whisk the sauce until it is thick and foamy. Serve at once with steamed or baked puddings, ice cream, fruit pies or stewed fruit.

# Coffee Cream Sauce

Makes about 275 ml/$\frac{1}{2}$ pt/$1\frac{1}{4}$ cups

|  | Metric | Imperial | American |
|---|---|---|---|
| Dried egg powder | 60 ml | 4 tbls | 4 tbls |
| Water | 120 ml | 8 tbls | 8 tbls |
| Instant coffee | 15 ml | 1 tbls | 1 tbls |
| Caster sugar | 50 g | 2 oz | $\frac{1}{4}$ cup |
| Double cream | 150 ml | $\frac{1}{4}$ pt | $\frac{2}{3}$ cup |

1. Blend the dried egg and water to a smooth cream in a basin. Stir in the coffee and place the basin over a pan of boiling water. Add the sugar. Cook, stirring occasionally, until the sauce is thick enough to coat the back of a wooden spoon lightly.

2. Remove the basin from the heat and cool, stirring occasionally. Chill.

3. Whip the cream until thick, then fold into the sauce. Serve chilled with steamed puddings or cold desserts.

# Custard Sauce

Makes about 275 ml/½ pt/1¼ cups

|  | Metric | Imperial | American |
|---|---|---|---|
| *Dried egg powder* | *60 ml* | *4 tbls* | *4 tbls* |
| *Water* | *60 ml* | *4 tbls* | *4 tbls* |
| *Vanilla essence* | *5 ml* | *1 tsp* | *1 tsp* |
| *Caster sugar* | *15 ml* | *1 tbls* | *1 tbls* |
| *Milk* | *275 ml* | *½ pt* | *1¼ cups* |

1. Blend the dried egg and water to a smooth cream. Stir in the vanilla essence and sugar.

2. Heat the milk almost to boiling point in a small saucepan. Stir into the egg mixture. Whisk well. Return to the rinsed-out saucepan.

3. Cook the sauce over a very low heat, stirring with a wooden spoon, until the sauce thickens enough to coat the back of the spoon. Serve warm or cold.

## Variations

*Chocolate Custard Sauce:*   Add 10 ml/2 tsp of cocoa powder to the egg mixture and mix well.

*Orange Custard Sauce:*   Omit the vanilla essence and add 5 ml/1 tsp of grated orange rind to the egg mixture with the milk.

# DESSERTS

It is in puddings and desserts which most people find they use lightly cooked eggs the most. Everything from those popular nursery favourites, Crème Caramel and Bread and Butter Pudding to the classic dinner party desserts like Cold Lemon Soufflé and Chocolate Pots include eggs. The recipes in this chapter are just as delicious as their fresh egg cousins.

# Bread and Butter Pudding

Serves 4 to 6

|  | Metric | Imperial | American |
|---|---|---|---|
| *Thin slices of white bread* | 5 | 5 | 5 |
| *Softened butter* | 40 g | $1\frac{1}{2}$ oz | 3 tbls |
| *Grated rind of $\frac{1}{2}$ lemon* |  |  |  |
| *Sultanas* | 100 g | 4 oz | $\frac{3}{4}$ cup |
| *Dried egg powder* | 75 ml | 5 tbls | 5 tbls |
| *Water* | 75 ml | 5 tbls | 5 tbls |
| *Milk* | 425 ml | $\frac{3}{4}$ pt | 2 cups |
| *Caster sugar* | 40 g | $1\frac{1}{2}$ oz | 3 tbls |
| *Grated nutmeg* |  |  |  |

1. Remove the crusts from the bread. Spread the slices with softened butter and cut each slice into 4 triangles. Arrange the slices in a buttered 1.15 1/2 pt/5 cup ovenproof dish, in layers with the lemon rind and sultanas.

2. Blend the dried egg and water to a smooth cream. Heat the milk and sugar until the sugar dissolves, then pour it on to the egg, stirring continuously. Pour over the bread. Sprinkle with a little nutmeg.

3. Place the dish in a roasting tin and add warm water to come halfway up side of dish.

4. Cook the pudding in the centre of a moderate oven at 160°C/325°F/Gas mark 3 until the custard is set and the pudding lightly browned, about 1 hour.

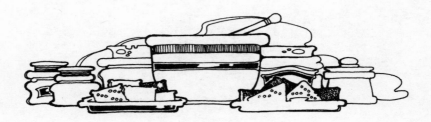

# Lemon Sauce Pudding

Serves 4

|  | Metric | Imperial | American |
| --- | --- | --- | --- |
| *Lemon* | *1* | *1* | *1* |
| *Dried egg powder* | *30 ml* | *2 tbls* | *2 tbls* |
| *Water* | *45 ml* | *3 tbls* | *3 tbls* |
| *Butter* | *50 g* | *2 oz* | *$\frac{1}{4}$ cup* |
| *Caster sugar* | *100 g* | *4 oz* | *$\frac{1}{2}$ cup* |
| *Plain flour* | *50 g* | *2 oz* | *$\frac{1}{4}$ cup* |
| *Milk* | *150 ml* | *$\frac{1}{4}$ pt* | *$\frac{2}{3}$ cup* |
| *Dried egg white* | *15 ml* | *1 tbls* | *1 tbls* |
| *Water* | *60 ml* | *4 tbls* | *4 tbls* |

1. Grate the rind and squeeze the juice from the lemon. Blend the dried egg and 45 ml/3 tbls of water to a smooth cream.

2. Cream the butter and sugar together until light in colour. Beat in the blended egg. Stir in the flour, lemon rind and juice, and milk.

3. Blend the egg white and 15 ml/1 tbls of water together, then stir in the remaining water. Whisk until stiff. Fold into the lemon mixture and pour into a buttered 900 ml/1$\frac{1}{2}$ pt/3$\frac{3}{4}$ cup ovenproof dish.

4. Bake in the centre of a moderate oven at 180°C/350°F/Gas mark 4 for about 40 minutes, until risen and golden brown. The pudding will have a layer of lemon sauce under a light sponge top.

# Lemon Meringue Pie

Serves 4 to 6

|  | Metric | Imperial | American |
|---|---|---|---|
| **Pastry** | | | |
| Plain flour | 225 g | 8 oz | 2 cups |
| Salt | 2.5 ml | $\frac{1}{2}$ tsp | $\frac{1}{2}$ tsp |
| Lard or white fat | 50 g | 2 oz | $\frac{1}{4}$ cup |
| Butter or margarine | 50 g | 2 oz | $\frac{1}{4}$ cup |
| Water (approximately) | 30 ml | 2 tbls | 2 tbls |
| **Filling** | | | |
| Small lemons | 2 | 2 | 2 |
| Cornflour | 30 ml | 2 tbls | 2 tbls |
| Caster sugar | 60 ml | 4 tbls | 4 tbls |
| Water | 275 ml | $\frac{1}{2}$ pt | $1\frac{1}{4}$ cups |
| Dried egg powder | 45 ml | 3 tbls | 3 tbls |
| Water | 45 ml | 3 tbls | 3 tbls |
| **Meringue** | | | |
| Dried egg white | 30 ml | 2 tbls | 2 tbls |
| Water | 120 ml | 8 tbls | 8 tbls |
| Caster sugar | 150 g | 5 oz | $\frac{2}{3}$ cup |

1. Sift the flour and salt into a bowl. Add the fats cut into small pieces and rub in with the fingertips until the mixture resembles fine breadcrumbs. Add sufficient water to form a firm dough. Knead lightly.

2. Roll out the pastry and use to line a 20 cm/8 in flan ring on a baking sheet. Line the flan with foil or greaseproof paper and weigh down with baking beans. Bake in the centre of a moderately hot oven at 200°C/400°F/Gas mark 6 for 15 minutes. Remove the beans and foil or paper and return to the oven for a further 5 minutes to dry the centre.

3. Grate the rind and the squeeze juice from the lemons. Place in a small saucepan with the cornflour and sugar and mix to a smooth cream. Gradually blend in the water. Bring to the boil, stirring, and cook for 2 minutes until thick.

4. Blend the dried egg and water together to a smooth cream, stir in a little of the lemon sauce, then whisk the egg mixture into the remaining lemon sauce. Leave to cool slightly, then pour into the pastry case.

5. Blend the egg white and 30 ml/2 tbls of water together until smooth. Gradually mix in the remaining water and whisk until stiff. Fold in the sugar lightly but thoroughly. Pile on top of the lemon mixture to cover the filling. Bake in the centre of a cool oven at 150°C/300°F/Gas mark 2 for 20 to 30 minutes until the meringue is crisp and golden. Serve warm.

# Zabaglione

Serves 3 to 4

|                          | Metric  | Imperial | American        |
| ------------------------ | ------- | -------- | --------------- |
| Dried egg powder         | 60 ml   | 4 tbls   | 4 tbls          |
| Marsala or medium sherry | 120 ml  | 8 tbls   | 8 tbls          |
| Caster sugar             | 75 g    | 3 oz     | $\frac{1}{3}$ cup |
| Finely grated lemon rind | 5 ml    | 1 tsp    | 1 tsp           |
| Dried egg white          | 15 ml   | 1 tbls   | 1 tbls          |
| Water                    | 60 ml   | 4 tbls   | 4 tbls          |

1. Blend the dried egg and marsala or sherry to a smooth cream in a medium-sized bowl. Stir in the sugar. Place the bowl over a saucepan of gently boiling water and stir occasionally until the mixture thickens slightly.

2. Blend the egg white and 15 ml/1 tbls of water until smooth. Stir in the remaining water and whisk until stiff. Fold the egg white into the custard in the bowl and continue cooking, stirring gently, for a further 2 minutes.

3. Spoon into dessert glasses and serve warm with crisp biscuits.

# Hot Chocolate Soufflés

Serves 4

|  | Metric | Imperial | American |
|---|---|---|---|
| *Dried egg powder* | *45 ml* | *3 tbls* | *3 tbls* |
| *Water* | *45 ml* | *3 tbls* | *3 tbls* |
| *Caster sugar* | *50 g* | *2 oz* | *$\frac{1}{4}$ cup* |
| *Butter or margarine* | *25 g* | *1 oz* | *2 tbls* |
| *Plain flour* | *25 g* | *1 oz* | *$\frac{1}{4}$ cup* |
| *Milk* | *150 ml* | *$\frac{1}{4}$ pt* | *$\frac{2}{3}$ cup* |
| *Plain chocolate* | *75 g* | *3 oz* | *3 oz* |
| *Dried egg white* | *30 ml* | *2 tbls* | *2 tbls* |
| *Water* | *120 ml* | *8 tbls* | *8 tbls* |
| *Icing sugar* | | | |

1. Lightly butter 4 individual soufflé dishes (150 ml/$\frac{1}{4}$ pt/$\frac{2}{3}$ cup capacity).

2. Blend the dried egg and water to a smooth cream. Stir in the sugar. Melt the butter or margarine in a saucepan, stir in the flour and cook for 2 minutes. Gradually blend in the milk and bring to the boil. Cook for 2 minutes. Cool slightly. Chop the chocolate and stir into the sauce. Stir until melted. Stir in the egg mixture.

3. Blend the egg white with 30 ml/2 tbls of water until smooth. Gradually blend in the remaining water. Whisk until stiff.

4. Add a spoonful of the egg whites to the chocolate mixture and mix well. Fold the chocolate mixture into the egg whites, lightly but thoroughly. Divide between the soufflé dishes.

5. Cook in a moderately hot oven at 200°C/400°F/Gas mark 6 for 15 to 20 minutes until risen and browned. Dust with icing sugar and serve at once.

# Apple Princess Pudding

Serves 4

|  | Metric | Imperial | American |
| --- | --- | --- | --- |
| Cooking apples | 450 g | 1 lb | 1 lb |
| Water | 45 ml | 3 tbls | 3 tbls |
| Butter or margarine | 25 g | 1 oz | 2 tbls |
| Caster sugar | 50 g | 2 oz | $\frac{1}{4}$ cup |
| Sponge finger biscuits, coarsely chopped | 10 | 10 | 10 |
| Ground cinnamon | 5 ml | 1 tsp | 1 tsp |
| **Topping** | | | |
| Dried egg white | 15 ml | 1 tbls | 1 tbls |
| Water | 60 ml | 4 tbls | 4 tbls |
| Caster sugar | 75 g | 3 oz | $\frac{1}{3}$ cup |
| Granulated sugar | 10 ml | 2 tsp | 2 tsp |

1. Peel, core and slice the apples. Put in a saucepan with the water. Cover and cook over a low heat until the apples are very soft. Beat to a pulp.

2. Stir the butter, sugar, chopped sponge fingers and cinnamon into the apple. Mix well and turn into a 750 ml/1$\frac{1}{4}$ pt/3 cup ovenproof dish.

3. Blend the egg white with 15 ml/1 tbls of water until smooth. Stir in the remaining water and whisk until stiff. Whisk in the sugar and whisk again until stiff. Spread over the apple mixture. Sprinkle with granulated sugar and bake in the centre of a moderate oven at 160°C/325°F/Gas mark 3 for about 40 minutes or until the meringue is crisp and brown. Serve hot with single cream.

# Queen of Puddings

Serves 4

|  | Metric | Imperial | American |
|---|---|---|---|
| Fresh white breadcrumbs | 75 g | 3 oz | $1\frac{1}{2}$ cups |
| Caster sugar | 25 g | 1 oz | 2 tbls |
| Lemon rind | 5 ml | 1 tsp | 1 tsp |
| Dried egg powder | 60 ml | 4 tbls | 4 tbls |
| Water | 60 ml | 4 tbls | 4 tbls |
| Milk | 425 ml | $\frac{3}{4}$ pt | 2 cups |
| Butter or margarine | 25 g | 1 oz | 2 tbls |
| Jam or marmalade | 45 ml | 3 tbls | 3 tbls |
| **Topping** | | | |
| Dried egg white | 15 ml | 1 tbls | 1 tbls |
| Water | 60 ml | 4 tbls | 4 tbls |
| Caster sugar | 75 g | 3 oz | $\frac{1}{3}$ cup |
| Granulated sugar | 10 ml | 2 tsp | 2 tsp |

1. Put the breadcrumbs, caster sugar and lemon rind in a bowl and mix well. Blend the dried egg and water to a smooth cream.

2. Heat the milk and butter or margarine until the butter melts. Pour on to the egg mixture and stir well. Pour on to the breadcrumb mixture and turn into a 750 ml/ $1\frac{1}{2}$ pt/$3\frac{3}{4}$ cup buttered ovenproof dish. Leave to stand for 30 minutes.

3. Bake the pudding in the centre of a moderate oven at 160°C/325°F/Gas mark 3, until set, about 1 hour. Cool for 30 minutes. Spread the jam or marmalade over the top of the pudding.

4. Blend the egg white and 15 ml/1 tbls of the water until smooth. Stir in the remaining water and whisk until stiff. Whisk in half the caster sugar, then fold in the remainder. Spread over the pudding and sprinkle with granulated sugar.

5. Return to the oven and cook until the meringue is crisp and beginning to brown, about 30 minutes longer. Serve hot.

# Jam Soufflé Omelette

Serves 2

|  | Metric | Imperial | American |
| --- | --- | --- | --- |
| Dried egg powder | 45 ml | 3 tbls | 3 tbls |
| Water | 45 ml | 3 tbls | 3 tbls |
| Caster sugar | 25 g | 1 oz | 2 tbls |
| Vanilla essence | 2.5 ml | $\frac{1}{2}$ tsp | $\frac{1}{2}$ tsp |
| Dried egg white | 30 ml | 2 tbls | 2 tbls |
| Water | 120 ml | 8 tbls | 8 tbls |
| Butter | 25 g | 1 oz | 2 tbls |
| Jam, warmed | 30 ml | 2 tbls | 2 tbls |

1. Blend the dried egg and water to a smooth cream. Stir in the sugar and vanilla essence.

2. Blend the egg white and 30 ml/2 tbls of the water until smooth. Stir in the remaining water and whisk until stiff. Fold in the egg mixture, lightly but thoroughly.

3. Prepare a hot grill. Heat the butter in a large frying pan. When hot, pour in the egg mixture and cook for about 3 minutes, until golden underneath. Place the pan under the grill and cook until the omelette is risen and golden brown on top. Quickly spread the jam over the omelette. Slide on to a warm serving plate, folding the omelette in half. Sprinkle the top with a little extra sugar, if liked, and serve at once.

# Baked Alaska

Serves 4 to 6

|  | Metric | Imperial | American |
| --- | --- | --- | --- |
| 18 cm/7 in Victoria sandwich layer (see page123) | 1 | 1 | 1 |
| Brandy, (optional) | 15 ml | 1 tbls | 1 tbls |
| Ice cream (any flavour) | 550 ml | 1 pt | $2\frac{1}{2}$ cups |
| Dried egg white | 30 ml | 2 tbls | 2 tbls |
| Water | 120 ml | 8 tbls | 8 tbls |
| Caster sugar | 150 g | 5 oz | $\frac{2}{3}$ cup |

1. Place the sandwich layer on a flat ovenproof dish which leaves a border of at least 2.5 cm/1 in all round. A baking sheet may be used but it is difficult to transfer the dessert on to a dish after cooking. Sprinkle the cake with brandy, if using.

2. Mould the ice cream into a dome shape on the cake, leaving a 2.5 cm/1 in border of cake all round. Keep in the freezer until ready to use.

3. Prepare a very hot oven to 230°C/450°F/Gas mark 8.

4. Blend the egg white and 30 ml/2 tbls of water until smooth. Stir in the remaining water and whisk until stiff. Fold in the sugar, reserving 10 ml/2 tsp for sprinkling.

5. Quickly spread the meringue over the ice cream and cake, making sure it is an even thickness and that no ice cream is uncovered. Sprinkle with the reserved sugar.

6. Bake the Alaska in the centre of the prepared oven for 3 to 5 minutes until the meringue is brown. Serve at once.

# Chocolate Pots

Serves 4

|  | Metric | Imperial | American |
|---|---|---|---|
| *Plain chocolate* | *100 g* | *4 oz* | *$\frac{1}{4}$ lb* |
| *Dried egg powder* | *60 ml* | *4 tbls* | *4 tbls* |
| *Water* | *45 ml* | *3 tbls* | *3 tbls* |
| *Whisky, rum or brandy* | *30 ml* | *2 tbls* | *2 tbls* |
| *Dried egg white* | *15 ml* | *1 tbls* | *1 tbls* |
| *Water* | *45 ml* | *3 tbls* | *3 tbls* |

**1.** Break up the chocolate and place in a bowl over a pan of hot, but not boiling water. Leave until melted. (Alternatively, place the chocolate in a bowl and heat in a microwave on DEFROST until melted.)

**2.** Blend the egg powder, water and whisky, rum or brandy to a smooth cream. Stir into the melted chocolate. Stir over the heat for 3 minutes (or microwave on DEFROST for 2 minutes). Remove from the heat.

**3.** Blend the egg white powder with a little water to a smooth paste, then gradually blend in the remaining water. Whisk until very stiff. Fold into the chocolate mixture.

**4.** Spoon the chocolate into small ramekins or dishes and leave to set. Chill in the refrigerator, preferably overnight.

# Baked Bistro Cheesecake

Serves 6 to 8

|  | Metric | Imperial | American |
|---|---|---|---|
| *Nice biscuits* | *175 g* | *6 oz* | *6 oz* |
| *Walnuts, chopped* | *25 g* | *1 oz* | *¼ cup* |
| *Demerara sugar* | *25 g* | *1 oz* | *2 tbls* |
| *Butter or margarine* | *75 g* | *3 oz* | *⅓ cup* |
| *Cream cheese* | *450 g* | *1 lb* | *2 cups* |
| *Caster sugar* | *175 g* | *6 oz* | *¾ cup* |
| *Lemon rind* | *5 ml* | *1 tsp* | *1 tsp* |
| *Lemon juice* | *15 ml* | *1 tbls* | *1 tbls* |
| *Dried egg powder* | *60 ml* | *4 tbls* | *4 tbls* |
| *Water* | *90 ml* | *6 tbls* | *6 tbls* |
| *Soured cream* | *150 ml* | *5 fl oz* | *⅔ cup* |
| *Grated nutmeg* |  |  |  |

1. Crush the biscuits in a paper bag with a rolling pin, then mix with the walnuts and Demerara sugar. Melt the butter in a small saucepan, add the biscuits and mix well. Press into the bottom and up the sides of an 18 cm/7 in loose-bottomed cake tin. Chill while preparing the filling.

2. Cream the cheese and caster sugar together. Stir in the lemon rind and juice.

3. Blend the dried egg and water to a smooth cream, then stir in the soured cream. Reserve 3 tablespoons of this mixture for topping, and stir the remainder into the cheese mixture. Turn into the biscuit-lined tin and level the top. Bake in a moderate oven at 160°C/325°F/Gas mark 3 for 1½ hours. The cheesecake should be set on top but still soft inside. Turn off the oven. Pour the reserved soured cream and egg mixture on top and leave the cheesecake to cool in the cooling oven.

4. Run a knife around the cheesecake to loosen it from the tin, then push it out of the tin and place on a serving dish. Sprinkle the nutmeg over the top before serving.

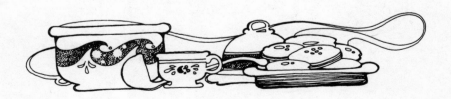

# Chilled Orange Cheesecake

Serves 6 to 8

|  | Metric | Imperial | American |
|---|---|---|---|
| Digestive biscuits | 175 g | 6 oz | 6 oz |
| Butter | 75 g | 3 oz | $\frac{1}{3}$ cup |
| Demerara sugar | 25 g | 1 oz | 2 tbls |
| Envelope of gelatine | 1 | 1 | 1 |
| Fresh orange juice | 150 ml | $\frac{1}{4}$ pt | $\frac{2}{3}$ cup |
| Curd cheese | 225 g | 8 oz | 1 cup |
| Cream cheese | 225 g | 8 oz | 1 cup |
| Caster sugar | 100 g | 4 oz | $\frac{1}{2}$ cup |
| Grated orange rind | 15 ml | 1 tbls | 1 tbls |
| Dried egg white | 15 ml | 1 tbls | 1 tbls |
| Water | 75 ml | 5 tbls | 5 tbls |

Fresh or jelly orange slices to decorate

1. Place the biscuits in paper bag and crush finely with a rolling pin. Melt the butter, stir in the crushed biscuits and Demerara sugar. Mix well and press into the bottom of a 20 cm/8 in loose-bottomed cake tin.

2. Sprinkle the gelatine over the orange juice in a bowl. Place over a saucepan of boiling water and stir occasionally until the gelatine has dissolved. (Alternatively place the bowl in a microwave oven on DEFROST setting until the gelatine has dissolved.) Leave to cool.

3. Cream the curd cheese, cream cheese and sugar together until smooth. Stir in the orange rind.

4. Mix the dried egg white and half the water until smooth, then gradually blend in the remaining water. Whisk until stiff.

5. Stir the cooled gelatine mixture into the cheeses, then lightly fold in the whisked egg white. Turn into the tin, level the top and chill until firm.

6. To serve, loosen the cheesecake from the sides of the tin with a knife, then push up the base and place the cheesecake on a dish. Decorate with fresh or jelly orange slices.

## Variation
Any citrus juice and rind may be substituted for the orange. Mandarin and clementine are particularly good. If using lemon, lime or grapefruit, increase the caster sugar to taste.

# Rhubarb Fool

Serves 4

|  | Metric | Imperial | American |
|---|---|---|---|
| Rhubarb | 900 g | 2 lb | 2 lb |
| Dried egg powder | 60 ml | 4 tbls | 4 tbls |
| Caster sugar | 100 g | 4 oz | $\frac{1}{2}$ cup |
| Water | 90 ml | 6 tbls | 6 tbls |
| Plain flour | 25 g | 1 oz | $\frac{1}{4}$ cup |
| Milk | 275 ml | $\frac{1}{2}$ pt | $1\frac{1}{4}$ cups |
| Vanilla pod OR | 1 | 1 | 1 |
| vanilla essence | 5 ml | 1 tsp | 1 tsp |
| Single cream to decorate |  |  |  |

1. Wash the rhubarb and cut into 4 cm/1$\frac{1}{2}$ in lengths. Place in a saucepan, cover with a close-fitting lid and cook over a gentle heat until soft. Shake the pan from time to time to prevent the rhubarb sticking. If very dry, add a drop of water but keep as dry as possible. (Alternatively place in a casserole, cover and cook in the microwave on HIGH for 12 to 15 minutes.)

2. Blend the egg powder, sugar and water to a smooth paste and mix well. Stir in the flour.

3. Heat the milk and vanilla pod or essence slowly. When just at boiling point, remove the vanilla pod, if using, and pour on to the egg mixture, stirring all the time. Pour back into the pan and bring to the boil, stirring constantly. Remove from the heat and leave to cool slightly.

4. Purée the rhubarb in a food processor or blender, then mix into the custard and pour into a serving dish. Leave to cool, then chill in the refrigerator. Swirl a little cream over the top before serving.

# Chocolate Roulade

Serve 6

|  | Metric | Imperial | American |
|---|---|---|---|
| Plain chocolate | 150 g | 5 oz | 5 oz |
| Hot water | 30 ml | 2 tbls | 2 tbls |
| Dried egg powder | 90 ml | 6 tbls | 6 tbls |
| Cold water | 90 ml | 6 tbls | 6 tbls |
| Caster sugar | 150 g | 5 oz | $\frac{2}{3}$ cup |
| Dried egg white | 60 ml | 4 tbls | 4 tbls |
| Cold water | 225 ml | 8 fl oz | 1 cup |
| Double cream | 150 ml | $\frac{1}{4}$ pt | $\frac{2}{3}$ cup |
| Rum | 15 ml | 1 tbls | 1 tbls |

Extra whipped cream and chocolate shapes
  for decoration (optional)

1. Grease a 38 x 23 cm/15 x 9 in Swiss roll tin and line with baking parchment.

2. Break up the chocolate and place in a bowl with the hot water, over a saucepan of hot, but not boiling, water. Stir occasionally until the chocolate has melted. (Alternatively, place the chocolate and water in a bowl in the microwave and heat on **DEFROST** until the chocolate has melted, stirring occasionally.)

3. Blend the dried egg and the 90 ml/6 tbls of cold water together until smooth. Stir in half the sugar, and stir into the melted chocolate.

4. Place the egg white in a bowl and add 60 ml/4 tbls of the water. Blend until smooth, then stir in the remaining water. Whisk until very stiff. Whisk in the remaining sugar. Fold lightly into the chocolate mixture and turn into the prepared tin. Level the top lightly and cook in a preheated oven at 180°C/350°F/Gas mark 4 for 15 to 20 minutes.

5. Remove from the oven and place the tin on a wire rack. Cover the roulade with a sheet of greaseproof paper and then a damp cloth and leave overnight.

6. Sprinkle a sheet of greaseproof paper with caster sugar. Turn out the roulade on to the paper and remove the baking parchment. Trim off any crisp edges.

7. Whisk the cream and rum until stiff and spread over the roulade. Holding one end of the greaseproof paper, carefully roll up the roulade like a Swiss roll. Place on a serving dish and decorate with more whipped cream and chocolate shapes, if liked.

# Custard Tart

Serves 4

|  | Metric | Imperial | American |
|---|---|---|---|
| **Pastry** | | | |
| Plain flour | 100 g | 4 oz | 1 cup |
| Margarine or butter | 25 g | 1 oz | 2 tbls |
| Lard or vegetable fat | 25 g | 1 oz | 2 tbls |
| Water | 20 ml | 4 tsp | 4 tsp |
| **Custard** | | | |
| Dried egg powder | 90 ml | 6 tbls | 6 tbls |
| Water | 90 ml | 6 tbls | 6 tbls |
| Caster sugar | 50 g | 2 oz | $\frac{1}{4}$ cup |
| Milk | 275 ml | $\frac{1}{2}$ pt | $1\frac{1}{4}$ cups |
| Vanilla essence | 5 ml | 1 tsp | 1 tsp |
| Grated nutmeg | | | |

1. Sift the flour into a bowl, add the fats cut into small pieces and rub in with the fingertips until the mixture resembles fine breadcrumbs. Add about 20 ml/4 tsp of water and mix to form a firm dough. Roll out the pastry on a floured surface and use to line an 18 cm/7 in flan dish.

2. Mix the dried egg and water to a smooth cream. Stir in the sugar. Heat the milk and vanilla essence until it is just boiling. Whisk into the egg mixture. Pour into the pastry-lined tin. Sprinkle a little grated nutmeg over the top of the custard.

3. Cook the tart in the centre of a moderately hot oven at 200°C/400°F/Gas mark 6 for 15 minutes. Reduce the temperature to 180°/350°F/Gas mark 4 and continue cooking until the custard is set and the pastry lightly browned, about 20 minutes. Serve warm or cold.

# Crême Caramel

Serves 4

|  | Metric | Imperial | American |
|---|---|---|---|
| **Caramel** | | | |
| Granulated sugar | 75 g | 3 oz | $\frac{1}{3}$ cup |
| Water | 45 ml | 3 tbls | 3 tbls |
| **Custard** | | | |
| Dried egg powder | 90 ml | 6 tbls | 6 tbls |
| Water | 135 ml | 9 tbls | 9 tbls |
| Caster sugar | 25 g | 1 oz | 2 tbls |
| Milk | 275 ml | $\frac{1}{2}$ pt | $1\frac{1}{4}$ cups |
| Single cream | 150 ml | $\frac{1}{4}$ pt | $\frac{2}{3}$ cup |
| Vanilla essence | 5 ml | 1 tsp | 1 tsp |

**1.** Warm a 750 ml/$1\frac{1}{4}$ pt/3 cup soufflé dish or ovenproof dish.

**2.** Place the sugar and water for the caramel in a heavy-based saucepan and heat slowly until the sugar has dissolved. Bring to the boil and boil rapidly until the sugar turns a deep golden brown. Quickly pour into the warmed dish and turn the dish to coat the base and sides with caramel.

**3.** Mix the dried egg and water to a smooth cream, then stir in the sugar. Heat the milk, cream and vanilla essence in the pan the caramel was made in until it is almost boiling, then pour on to the egg mixture, whisking lightly.

**4.** Pour the milk mixture into the caramel-lined dish. Place the dish in a roasting tin of warm water and cook in centre of a cool oven at 150°C/300°F/Gas mark 2 for about $1\frac{1}{2}$ hours or until set and lightly browned on top. Remove the dish from the oven and leave to cool. Chill. Turn out by loosening the edge of the custard with the point of a knife and inverting the dish on to a serving plate.

# Crême Brulée

Serves 4

|  | Metric | Imperial | American |
|---|---|---|---|
| Single cream | 425 ml | $\frac{3}{4}$ pt | 2 cups |
| Vanilla essence | 5 ml | 1 tsp | 1 tsp |
| Dried egg powder | 60 ml | 4 tbls | 4 tbls |
| Water | 120 ml | 8 tbls | 8 tbls |
| Caster sugar | 30 ml | 2 tbls | 2 tbls |
| Demerara sugar | 60 ml | 4 tbls | 4 tbls |

**1.** Heat the cream and vanilla essence until just about to boil.

**2.** Blend the dried egg and water to a smooth cream, then stir in the caster sugar. Pour on the hot cream, stirring all the time. Return to the pan and heat gently, stirring all the time with a wooden spoon until the custard thickens and coats the back of spoon. Do not allow to boil.

**3.** Pour the custard into 4 fireproof ramekin dishes and leave to cool. Chill.

**4.** Just before serving, sprinkle 15 ml/1 tbls of Demerara sugar over each dish to cover the custard completely. Place under a hot grill until the sugar caramelises.

## Variation

***Fruit Brulées:*** Place a little fruit – sliced strawberries, seeded grapes, orange segments, sliced apricots etc. – in the ramekins before pouring on the custard. A teaspoon of liqueur may be poured over the fruit, if liked.

# Charlotte Russe

Serves 6

|  | Metric | Imperial | American |
|---|---|---|---|
| Lemon jelly tablet | 1 | 1 | 1 |
| Boiling water |  |  |  |
| Glacé cherries | 6 | 6 | 6 |
| Angelica |  |  |  |
| Sponge finger biscuits | 16–18 | 16–18 | 16–18 |
| Envelope of gelatine | 1 | 1 | 1 |
| Water | 90 ml | 6 tbls | 6 tbls |
| Dried egg powder | 60 ml | 4 tbls | 4 tbls |
| Caster sugar | 50 g | 2 oz | $\frac{1}{4}$ cup |
| Milk | 275 ml | $\frac{1}{2}$ pt | $1\frac{1}{4}$ cups |
| Vanilla essence | 5 ml | 1 tsp | 1 tsp |
| Double cream | 250 ml | 8 fl oz | 1 cup |

1. Make up the jelly following the directions on the packet. Pour 150 ml/$\frac{1}{4}$ pt/$\frac{2}{3}$ cup into a 15 cm/6 in deep round cake tin or charlotte mould. Pour the remainder into a shallow dish. Leave to set.

2. Using halved or quartered glacé cherries and angelica cut into diamond shapes, make a decoration on the jelly which will look attractive when the charlotte is turned out.

3. Trim one end of the sponge finger biscuits with a sharp knife so they will stand firmly and arrange around the edge of the tin with the sugar side against the tin. Trim the sides of the biscuits if necessary with a sharp knife to get a good fit.

4. Sprinkle the gelatine over 30 ml/2 tbls of the water and leave to soak. Blend the dried egg and remaining water to a smooth cream. Stir in the sugar.

5. Heat the milk and vanilla essence in a small saucepan just to boiling point. Whisk on to the egg mixture. Return to the rinsed-out pan and cook over a low heat until the mixture thickens slightly. Do not allow to boil. Add the gelatine and stir until dissolved. Place the pan in a bowl of cold water and stir occasionally until just on the point of setting.

6. Whip the cream until stiff, fold into the custard mixture and turn at once into the lined tin. Leave to set, then chill.

7. To turn out the charlotte, dip the tin quickly in hot water and invert on to a serving dish. Chop the jelly set in the shallow dish and arrange around the base of the charlotte.

# Raspberry Soufflé

Serves 6

|                                        | Metric  | Imperial           | American             |
| -------------------------------------- | ------- | ------------------ | -------------------- |
| Fresh or frozen raspberries, thawed    | 450 g   | 1 lb               | 1 lb                 |
| Caster sugar                           | 100 g   | 4 oz               | $\frac{1}{2}$ cup    |
| Envelope of gelatine                   | 1       | 1                  | 1                    |
| Water                                  | 60 ml   | 4 tbls             | 4 tbls               |
| Dried egg white                        | 30 ml   | 2 tbls             | 2 tbls               |
| Water                                  | 120 ml  | 8 tbls             | 8 tbls               |
| Double cream                           | 275 ml  | $\frac{1}{2}$ pt   | $1\frac{1}{4}$ cups  |
| Chopped pistachio or other nuts        | 30 ml   | 2 tbls             | 2 tbls               |
| A few raspberries for decoration       |         |                    |                      |

1. Place a collar of greaseproof paper around a 900 ml/$1\frac{1}{2}$ pt/$3\frac{3}{4}$ cup soufflé dish to come 5 cm/2 in above the rim. Secure with string, pins or sticky tape.

2. Sieve the raspberries or purée in a food processor or blender, then sieve to remove the seeds. Stir in half the sugar.

3. Sprinkle the gelatine over the 60 ml/4 tbls of water in a basin and leave to soak for 5 minutes. Place the basin over a pan of hot water and stir the gelatine occasionally until dissolved. (Alternatively, dissolve the gelatine in a microwave oven on the DEFROST setting.)

4. Blend the egg white with 30 ml/2 tbls of water until smooth. Add the remaining water and whisk until stiff. Whisk in the remaining sugar.

5. Whip the cream until it just holds its shape. Reserve about 2 rounded tablespoons for decoration. Stir a little of the raspberry purée into the gelatine, mix well then stir in the remainder. Fold in the whisked egg white and cream lightly. Turn into the prepared dish, smooth the top and leave until set. Chill.

6. Carefully remove the paper collar from the soufflé dish and press the chopped nuts on to the side of soufflé. Decorate the top with piped rosettes of cream and raspberries.

## Variation

*Strawberry Soufflé:*   Replace the raspberries with strawberries and add 30 ml/2 tbls of lemon juice to the purée.

# Hazelnut Meringue

Serves 6 to 8

|  | Metric | Imperial | American |
|---|---|---|---|
| Hazelnuts | 100 g | 4 oz | $\frac{1}{4}$ lb |
| Dried egg white | 30 ml | 2 tbls | 2 tbls |
| Water | 120 ml | 8 tbls | 8 tbls |
| Caster sugar | 225 g | 8 oz | 1 cup |
| Double cream | 150 ml | $\frac{1}{4}$ pt | $\frac{2}{3}$ cup |
| Icing sugar |  |  |  |
| Soft fruit (optional) |  |  |  |

1. Brush two 20 cm/8 in sandwich tins with oil, line the bases with baking parchment and lightly oil the parchment.

2. Brown the hazelnuts under a medium grill or in the oven, rub off the skins, then chop the nuts finely.

3. Blend the egg white and 30 ml/2 tbls of the water until smooth, then blend in the remaining water. Whisk until very stiff. Whisk in the sugar, and continue whisking until the meringue becomes stiff and heavy. Fold in the chopped nuts and divide the mixture between the two tins. Level the tops.

4. Bake in the centre of a moderately hot oven at 190°C/375°F/Gas mark 5 for about 30 minutes until crisp and lightly browned. Cool in the tins for 10 minutes. Turn out, remove the parchment and leave to cool completely on a wire rack.

5. To serve, whip the cream until stiff and sandwich the meringues together with the cream. Place on a serving plate and dust with icing sugar. If liked, sliced strawberries or crushed raspberries may be spread over the cream before sandwiching the meringues together.

# Egg Nog Pie

Serves 6

|  | Metric | Imperial | American |
| --- | --- | --- | --- |
| **Pie crust** | | | |
| Gingernut biscuits | 175 g | 6 oz | 6 oz |
| Demerara sugar | 50 g | 2 oz | $\frac{1}{4}$ cup |
| Butter, melted | 75 g | 3 oz | $\frac{1}{3}$ cup |
| **Filling** | | | |
| Envelope of gelatine | 1 | 1 | 1 |
| Water | 90 ml | 6 tbls | 6 tbls |
| Dried egg powder | 60 ml | 4 tbls | 4 tbls |
| Rum | 30 ml | 2 tbls | 2 tbls |
| Caster sugar | 75 g | 3 oz | $\frac{1}{3}$ cup |
| Milk | 150 ml | $\frac{1}{4}$ pt | $\frac{2}{3}$ cup |
| Vanilla essence | 5 ml | 1 tsp | 1 tsp |
| Dried egg white | 15 ml | 1 tbls | 1 tbls |
| Water | 60 ml | 4 tbls | 4 tbls |
| Whipping cream | 150 ml | $\frac{1}{4}$ pt | $\frac{2}{3}$ cup |
| Grated nutmeg | | | |

1. Place the gingernuts in a paper bag and crush finely with a rolling pin. Combine with the caster sugar and melted butter. Press into the base and sides of a 20 cm/ 8 in flan dish and chill.

2. Sprinkle the gelatine over 30 ml/2 tbls of the water and leave to soak. Blend the dried egg and 60 ml/4 tbls of water to a smooth cream. Stir in the rum and half the caster sugar.

3. Place the milk and vanilla essence in a saucepan and bring just to boiling point. Whisk on to the egg mixture. Return to the rinsed-out saucepan and cook over a low heat until the mixture thickens slightly. Do not allow to boil. Add the gelatine and stir until dissolved. Place the saucepan in a bowl of cold water and stir occasionally until the mixture is just on the point of setting.

4. Blend the egg white and 15 ml/1 tbls of the water until smooth. Stir in the remaining water and whisk until stiff. Whisk in the remaining sugar.

5. Whip the cream until it will hold its shape. Fold the cooled custard into the egg white lightly, then fold in the cream. Leave until the mixture is partially set then pile into the pie crust. Leave to set completely. Sprinkle generously with grated nutmeg before serving.

# Strawberry Pavlova

Serves 4 to 6

|                  | Metric | Imperial          | American          |
| ---------------- | ------ | ----------------- | ----------------- |
| Dried egg white  | 30 ml  | 2 tbls            | 2 tbls            |
| Water            | 120 ml | 8 tbls            | 8 tbls            |
| Cornflour        | 5 ml   | 1 tsp             | 1 tsp             |
| Vinegar          | 5 ml   | 1 tsp             | 1 tsp             |
| Caster sugar     | 225 g  | 8 oz              | 1 cup             |
| Double cream     | 150 ml | $\frac{1}{4}$ pt  | $\frac{2}{3}$ cup |
| Strawberries     | 175 g  | 6 oz              | 6 oz              |

1. Line a baking sheet with baking parchment and brush very lightly with oil.

2. Blend the egg white and 30 ml/2 tbls of the water until smooth, then stir in the remaining water. Whisk until very stiff.

3. Combine the cornflour and vinegar and whisk into the egg white with the sugar. Spread in an even circle 2.5 cm/1 in thick on the parchment.

4. Cook in the centre of a cool oven at 140°C/275°F/Gas mark 1 for 1 hour. Turn off the oven and leave the Pavlova to cool in the oven.

5. Carefully peel the parchment from the Pavlova and place it on a serving dish.

6. Whip the cream until stiff. Spread on the Pavlova, leaving a 2.5 cm/1 in border all round. Hull the strawberries and pile on to the cream. Serve at once.

**Note**
The unfilled Pavlova will keep in an airtight container for 3 to 4 days.

# Meringues

Makes 12 shells

|  | Metric | Imperial | American |
|---|---|---|---|
| Dried egg white | 15 ml | 1 tbls | 1 tbls |
| Water | 60 ml | 4 tbls | 4 tbls |
| Caster sugar | 100 g | 4 oz | $\frac{1}{2}$ cup |

1. Blend the egg white and 15 ml/1 tbls of the water until smooth. Stir in the remaining water. Whisk until very stiff.

2. Whisk in half the sugar, then fold in the remainder, cutting through the meringue lightly with a metal spoon. Do not over mix.

3. Line a baking sheet with baking parchment. Spoon or pipe the meringue on to the baking parchment, making 12 equal-sized meringues.

4. Dry out the meringues in the centre of a very cool oven at 110°C/225°F/Gas mark $\frac{1}{4}$ for 2 to 3 hours or until the meringues will lift off the parchment easily. Cool, then sandwich together with whipped cream, if liked.

# Floating Islands

Serves 4

|  | Metric | Imperial | American |
|---|---|---|---|
| Dried egg white | 15 ml | 1 tbls | 1 tbls |
| Water | 60 ml | 4 tbls | 4 tbls |
| Caster sugar | 100 g | 4 oz | $\frac{1}{2}$ cup |
| Milk | 425 ml | $\frac{3}{4}$ pt | 2 cups |
| Dried egg powder | 60 ml | 4 tbls | 4 tbls |
| Water | 60 ml | 4 tbls | 4 tbls |
| Grated lemon rind | 5 ml | 1 tsp | 1 tsp |
| Sugared almonds | 8 | 8 | 8 |

1. Blend the egg white and 30 ml/2 tbls of the water until smooth. Stir in the remaining water and whisk until stiff. Whisk in 50 g/2 oz/$\frac{1}{4}$ cup of the sugar and continue whisking until the mixture stands in stiff peaks and looks glossy.

2. Heat the milk in a medium-sized saucepan almost to simmering point, but do not let it boil. Drop tablespoonsful of the egg white mixture into the milk and poach very gently for about 4 minutes, turning them over once. Lift out of the milk with a draining spoon and drain on kitchen paper whilst cooking the remaining egg white. The mixture should make 12 'islands' altogether.

3. Mix the dried egg powder and water to a smooth paste. Stir the remaining sugar and lemon rind into the dried egg mixture, pour on the hot milk and return to the rinsed-out saucepan. Heat over a low heat, stirring all the time until the custard thickens slightly (it will thicken more as it cools). Do not allow to boil. Cool slightly.

4. Divide the custard between 4 individual dessert glasses, arrange 3 poached meringues on each, cool, then chill. Serve topped with crushed sugared almonds.

# Honeycomb Mould

Serves 4

|  | Metric | Imperial | American |
|---|---|---|---|
| *Envelope of gelatine* | *1* | *1* | *1* |
| *Water* | *90 ml* | *6 tbls* | *6 tbls* |
| *Dried egg powder* | *30 ml* | *2 tbls* | *2 tbls* |
| *Caster sugar* | *50 g* | *2 oz* | *$\frac{1}{4}$ cup* |
| *Milk* | *600 ml* | *1 pt* | *$2\frac{1}{2}$ cups* |
| *Vanilla essence* | *5 ml* | *1 tsp* | *1 tsp* |
| *Dried egg white* | *15 ml* | *1 tbls* | *1 tbls* |
| *Water* | *60 ml* | *4 tbls* | *4 tbls* |

**1.** Sprinkle the gelatine on to 60 ml/4 tbls of the water and leave to soak.

**2.** Blend the dried egg and the remaining 30 ml/2 tbls of water to a smooth cream. Stir in half the sugar.

**3.** Heat the milk and vanilla essence in a medium-sized saucepan until just on the point of boiling. Stir into the egg mixture, return to pan and heat gently, stirring until the custard will coat the back of a wooden spoon thinly. Do not boil. Add the soaked gelatine and stir until dissolved.

**4.** Blend the egg white and 15 ml/1 tbls of water until smooth, stir in the remaining water and whisk until stiff. Whisk in the remaining sugar, and fold into the custard. Return to the heat, bring just to the boil.

**5.** Pour into a 1.15 litre/2 pt/5 cup mould which has been rinsed with cold water. Cool. Chill until set. The dessert will separate into layers when setting.

**6.** To turn out the mould, loosen around the top edge with the point of a knife, then dip the mould quickly into hot water and invert on to a dish.

# Cold Lemon Soufflé

Serves 4 to 6

|  | Metric | Imperial | American |
| --- | --- | --- | --- |
| *Lemons* | *2* | *2* | *2* |
| *Dried egg powder* | *45 ml* | *3 tbls* | *3 tbls* |
| *Water* | *90 ml* | *6 tbls* | *6 tbls* |
| *Envelope of gelatine* | *1* | *1* | *1* |
| *Caster sugar* | *175 g* | *6 oz* | *¾ cup* |
| *Dried egg white* | *30 ml* | *2 tbls* | *2 tbls* |
| *Water* | *120 ml* | *8 tbls* | *8 tbls* |
| *Double cream* | *225 ml* | *8 fl oz* | *1 cup* |
| *Chopped nuts to decorate* | *50 g* | *2 oz* | *½ cup* |
| *A little extra whipped cream* | | | |

1. Prepare a 750 ml/1¼ pt/3 cup soufflé dish by wrapping a double thickness band of greaseproof paper around the outside of the dish so that it stands 5 cm/2 in above the rim of the dish. Secure with pins, string or sticky tape. Make sure it is tight around the rim.

2. Grate the rind and squeeze the juice from the lemons. Blend the dried egg and 45 ml/3 tbls water to a smooth cream. Sprinkle the gelatine on to the remaining 45 ml/3 tbls of water and leave to soak.

3. Place the egg mixture, lemon rind and juice and sugar in a large bowl over a pan of boiling water and stir for 5 to 10 minutes, until mixture is hot and thickens slightly. Whisk in the soaked gelatine until it dissolves. Remove from the heat and leave to cool, until it is just on the point of setting.

4. Blend the egg white and 30 ml/2 tbls of water until smooth. Stir in the remaining water and whisk until stiff. Whip the cream until it just holds its shape.

5. Fold the cream and egg white into the lemon mixture and turn into the prepared soufflé dish. Chill until firm.

6. To finish the soufflé, carefully remove the paper collar from the soufflé and press the chopped nuts on to the edge. Decorate the top with whipped cream.

## Variations

*Chocolate Soufflé:* Omit the lemon rind and juice. Blend the dried egg powder with 45 ml/3 tbls of extra water and add 75 g/3 oz melted plain chocolate with the dissolved gelatine (method 3).

*Coffee Soufflé:* Omit the lemon rind and juice. Add the extra water to the dried egg as above and add 15 ml/1 tbls of instant coffee granules to the hot mixture.

*Orange Soufflé:* Replace the lemons with the rind and juice of 2 small oranges.

# Coffee Chiffon Pie

Serves 6

|  | Metric | Imperial | American |
|---|---|---|---|
| **Pie crust** |  |  |  |
| *Plain chocolate-covered digestive biscuits* | 175 g | 6 oz | 6 oz |
| *Caster sugar* | 50 g | 2 oz | $\frac{1}{4}$ cup |
| *Butter, melted* | 75 g | 3 oz | $\frac{1}{3}$ cup |
| **Filling** |  |  |  |
| *Envelope of gelatine* | 1 | 1 | 1 |
| *Water* | 90 ml | 6 tbls | 6 tbls |
| *Dried egg powder* | 60 ml | 4 tbls | 4 tbls |
| *Boiling water* | 150 ml | $\frac{1}{4}$ pt | $\frac{2}{3}$ cup |
| *Instant coffee* | 15 ml | 1 tbls | 1 tbls |
| *Caster sugar* | 100 g | 4 oz | $\frac{1}{2}$ cup |
| *Rum (optional)* | 30 ml | 2 tbls | 2 tbls |
| *Dried egg white* | 15 ml | 1 tbls | 1 tbls |
| *Water* | 60 ml | 4 tbls | 4 tbls |
| *Double cream* | 225 ml | 8 fl oz | 1 cup |

*A little extra cream and chocolate leaves or*
*vermicelli for decoration*

1. Place the biscuits in a paper bag and crush with a rolling pin to fairly fine crumbs. Combine with the sugar and melted butter. Press into the base and up the sides of a 20 cm/8 in flan dish to form a shell. Bake in a moderately hot oven at 190°C/375°F/Gas mark 5 for 8 minutes. Leave to cool completely.

2. Sprinkle the gelatine on to 30 ml/2 tbls of water and leave to soak. Blend the dried egg and 60 ml/4 tbls water to a smooth cream. Place the boiling water, coffee, half the sugar and the rum (if using) in a saucepan and bring to the boil. Whisk on to the egg mixture. Return to the saucepan and heat, stirring, until the mixture thickens slightly. Do not allow to boil. Remove from the heat, add the gelatine and stir until dissolved. Place the saucepan in a bowl of cold water and stir occasionally until the mixture is cool and just on the point of setting.

3. Blend the egg white and 15 ml/1 tbls of the water until smooth. Add the remaining water and whisk until very stiff. Whisk in the remaining sugar. Whip the cream until stiff. Lightly fold the coffee mixture into the egg whites, then fold in the cream. Leave for a few minutes to set partially. Pile into the cooled pie crust and leave to set completely.

4. Decorate with piped cream and chocolate leaves or vermicelli.

# St Emilion

Serves 6

|  | Metric | Imperial | American |
|---|---|---|---|
| Butter, softened | 150 g | 5 oz | $\frac{2}{3}$ cup |
| Icing sugar | 150 g | 5 oz | 1 cup |
| Dried egg powder | 15 ml | 1 tbls | 1 tbls |
| Water | 15 ml | 1 tbls | 1 tbls |
| Milk | 90 ml | 6 tbls | 6 tbls |
| White chocolate | 100 g | 4 oz | $\frac{1}{4}$ lb |
| Almond essence | 5 ml | 1 tsp | 1 tsp |
| Brandy or Ameretto di Saronno liqueur | 60 ml | 4 tbls | 4 tbls |
| Macaroons or ratafia biscuits | 225 g | 8 oz | $\frac{1}{2}$ lb |
| **Sauce** | | | |
| Plain chocolate | 50 g | 2 oz | 2 oz |
| Butter | 15 g | $\frac{1}{2}$ oz | 1 tbls |
| Water | 30 ml | 2 tbls | 2 tbls |

1. Cream the butter until very soft, add the icing sugar and cream again until soft.

2. Blend the dried egg and water to a smooth cream. Heat the milk until almost boiling, pour on to the egg mixture and stir well. Return to the pan and cook, stirring briskly for a minute, but do not allow to boil. Gradually blend into the butter mixture.

3. Break up the chocolate and place in a bowl over a pan of hot, but not boiling water. Stir occasionally until melted. (Alternatively, place in a microwave oven on DEFROST setting and heat until melted.) It is very important not to overheat white chocolate or it may go fudgy. Stir the melted chocolate into the butter mixture with the almond essence.

4. Pour the brandy or liqueur into a shallow dish. Line a 450 g/1 lb loaf tin with baking parchment. Dip the macaroons or ratafias into the brandy or liqueur and line the base and sides of the tin, with the rounded sides against the tin. Spoon the chocolate mixture into the tin and level the top. Place the remaining macaroons or ratafias on top. Cover and chill the dessert. (It may be frozen for up to 6 weeks.)

5. To make the sauce, place the plain chocolate, butter and water in a small bowl over a pan of hot water and stir occasionally until melted.

6. Turn out the dessert on to a serving dish, remove the paper and spoon the sauce over the dessert so it trickles down the sides. Serve chilled.

# Vanilla Ice Cream

Serves 6

|  | Metric | Imperial | American |
|---|---|---|---|
| Milk | 150 ml | $\frac{1}{4}$ pt | $\frac{2}{3}$ cup |
| Vanilla pod OR | 1 | 1 | 1 |
| vanilla essence | 5 ml | 1 tsp | 1 tsp |
| Dried egg powder | 60 ml | 4 tbls | 4 tbls |
| Water | 60 ml | 4 tbls | 4 tbls |
| Caster sugar | 75 g | 3 oz | $\frac{1}{3}$ cup |
| Double cream | 275 ml | $\frac{1}{2}$ pt | $1\frac{1}{4}$ cups |
| Dried egg white | 30 ml | 1 tbls | 1 tbls |
| Water | 60 ml | 4 tbls | 4 tbls |

**1.** Heat the milk and vanilla pod or essence together until it just comes to the boil.

**2.** Meanwhile, mix the dried egg and 60 ml/4 tbls of water together, then mix in the sugar. Pour on the milk, stirring, then return the mixture to the saucepan and heat gently, until it thickens enough to coat the back of a wooden spoon. Do not let the custard boil. Cool.

**3.** Whisk the cream until it will hold its shape. Blend the egg white powder and half the water until smooth. Gradually add the remaining water and whisk until stiff. Fold the cream and egg white into the cooled custard. Turn into a freezer tray or dish and freeze until the mixture has frozen 2.5 cm/1 in from the sides of the dish. Turn into a chilled bowl and whisk until smooth. Put back into the dish and freeze until firm.

## Variations

***Ginger Ice Cream:***   Add 6 pieces of finely chopped stem ginger when whisking the partially frozen ice cream.

***Brown Bread Ice Cream:***   Fry 75 g/3 oz/$\frac{3}{4}$ cup fresh brown breadcrumbs in 25 g/ 1 oz/2 tbls of butter until crisp and brown. Add 75 g/3 oz/$\frac{1}{3}$ cup of soft brown sugar and stir over a low heat until well mixed. Cool and add when whisking the partially frozen ice cream.

# Rich Butterscotch Ice Cream

Serves 4 to 6

|  | Metric | Imperial | American |
|---|---|---|---|
| *Soft light brown sugar* | *100 g* | *4 oz* | *$\frac{1}{2}$ cup* |
| *Water* | *150 ml* | *$\frac{1}{4}$ pt* | *$\frac{2}{3}$ cup* |
| *Dried egg powder* | *60 ml* | *4 tbls* | *4 tbls* |
| *Whipping cream* | *550 ml* | *1 pt* | *$2\frac{1}{2}$ cups* |

1. Put the sugar and 90 ml/6 tbls of the water in a saucepan and heat gently until the sugar has dissolved. Boil for 1 minute.

2. Blend the dried egg with the remaining water to a smooth cream. Pour on the sugar syrup, whisking all the time.

3. Lightly whip the cream until it will just hold its shape. Fold in the egg mixture. Turn into a dish and freeze until frozen 2.5 cm/1 in in from the edges. Turn into a bowl and whisk well. Return to the dish and freeze until firm.

**Note**
If using an ice cream making machine, do not whip the cream, or it may over-whip whilst the paddles are churning. Chill the cream mixture before putting it in the machine.

# Fruit Sorbet

Serves 4 to 6

|  | Metric | Imperial | American |
|---|---|---|---|
| Water | 275 ml | $\frac{1}{2}$ pt | $1\frac{1}{4}$ cups |
| Granulated sugar | 100 g | 4 oz | $\frac{1}{2}$ cup |
| Unsweetened fruit purée | 275 ml | $\frac{1}{2}$ pt | $1\frac{1}{4}$ cups |
| Dried egg white | 15 ml | 1 tbls | 1 tbls |
| Water | 60 ml | 4 tbls | 4 tbls |

**1.** Place the water and sugar in a saucepan. Heat gently until the sugar has dissolved, then bring to the boil and boil steadily for 5 minutes.

**2.** Add the fruit purée to the syrup and leave to cool. It may be any unsweetened purée such as raspberry, blackcurrant, plum or strawberry. If using strawberry, add 30 ml/2 tbls of lemon juice.

**3.** When quite cold, freeze the purée until slushy. Blend the egg white with 15 ml/1 tbls of the water until smooth, then stir in the remaining water and whisk until very stiff. Fold into the partially frozen sorbet, return to the freezer and freeze until firm.

# ICINGS AND SWEETS

Whilst cake icings and fillings are not made every day and home made sweets are for festive occasions, these recipes will enable you to make gifts for family and friends with perfect peace of mind.

# Royal Icing

Makes sufficient to ice the top and sides of a 20 cm/8 in cake with 2 coats of icing

|  | Metric | Imperial | American |
|---|---|---|---|
| Icing sugar | 1 kg | $2\frac{1}{4}$ lb | $6\frac{3}{4}$ cups |
| Dried egg white | 45 ml | 3 tbls | 3 tbls |
| Water (approximately) | 225 ml | 8 fl oz | 1 cup |
| Glycerine (optional) | 10 ml | 2 tsp | 2 tsp |

1. Sift the icing sugar into a bowl. Blend the egg white with 45 ml/3 tbls of the water until smooth. Gradually blend in all but 15 ml/1 tbls of the remaining water. Add to the icing sugar and beat very well until the icing stands up in stiff peaks.

2. Add the glycerine, if liked, to prevent the icing becoming too hard. Do not add glycerine if using the icing for piping. Add the remaining water, if required, to give the right consistency.

3. Cover the bowl with a damp cloth and leave for an hour to let the bubbles rise. Use to ice the cake.

# American Frosting

Makes sufficient to cover an 18 cm/7 in cake

|                 | Metric | Imperial | American |
|-----------------|--------|----------|----------|
| Dried egg white | 15 ml  | 1 tbls   | 1 tbls   |
| Water           | 60 ml  | 4 tbls   | 4 tbls   |
| Caster sugar    | 175 g  | 6 oz     | $\frac{3}{4}$ cup |

1. Blend the egg white and 15 ml/1 tbls of the water in a basin until smooth. Stir in the remaining water and the sugar.

2. Place the basin over a saucepan of boiling water and whisk with an electric mixer for about 5 minutes or until the mixture thickens.

3. Remove the bowl from the heat and whisk for a few minutes more, then spread quickly over the cake and leave to set.

# Chocolate Fudge Frosting

Makes enough to ice an 18 cm/7 in cake

|  | Metric | Imperial | American |
|---|---|---|---|
| Packet plain chocolate chips | 1 | 1 | 1 |
| Butter | 50 g | 2 oz | $\frac{1}{4}$ cup |
| Dried egg powder | 30 ml | 2 tbls | 2 tbls |
| Water | 45 ml | 3 tbls | 3 tbls |
| Icing sugar | 225 g | 8 oz | $1\frac{1}{2}$ cups |

1. Place the chocolate chips and butter in a bowl over a pan of hot, but not boiling, water. Stir occasionally until melted. (Alternatively melt the chocolate in a bowl in a microwave oven on DEFROST.)

2. Blend the dried egg and water to a smooth cream. When the chocolate has melted, stir in the egg mixture. Remove from the heat and add the sifted icing sugar. Beat for a few minutes.

3. Spread the icing over the top and sides of the cake and swirl with a round-ended knife. Leave to set.

# Almond Paste

Sufficient to cover top and sides of 15 cm/6 in cake

|  | Metric | Imperial | American |
|---|---|---|---|
| Ground almonds | 225 g | 8 oz | 2 cups |
| Icing sugar, sifted | 100 g | 4 oz | $\frac{3}{4}$ cup |
| Caster sugar | 100 g | 4 oz | $\frac{1}{2}$ cup |
| Dried egg powder | 30 ml | 2 tbls | 2 tbls |
| Water | 30 ml | 2 tbls | 2 tbls |
| Lemon juice | 15 ml | 1 tbls | 1 tbls |
| Almond essence | 5 ml | 1 tsp | 1 tsp |

**1.** Combine the almonds and both sugars in a bowl. Blend the egg powder and water to a smooth cream. Make a well in the centre of the almond mixture and add the egg, lemon juice and almond essence.

**2.** Gradually blend the almond mixture into the liquid with a wooden spoon. When fairly firm knead with the hands to make a smooth pliable paste. Do not over knead or the paste will become oily. Use to cover a cake or make into sweets.

# Confectioners' Custard

Makes sufficient to fill and top a 20 cm/8 in cake

|  | Metric | Imperial | American |
|---|---|---|---|
| *Dried egg powder* | *45 ml* | *3 tbls* | *3 tbls* |
| *Plain flour* | *25 g* | *1 oz* | *$\frac{1}{4}$ cup* |
| *Caster sugar* | *50 g* | *2 oz* | *$\frac{1}{4}$ cup* |
| *Water* | *60 ml* | *4 tbls* | *4 tbls* |
| *Milk* | *275 ml* | *$\frac{1}{2}$ pt* | *$1\frac{1}{4}$ cups* |
| *Vanilla pod OR* |  |  |  |
| *vanilla essence* | *5 ml* | *1 tsp* | *1 tsp* |

1. Mix the dried egg, flour and sugar in a basin, then blend in the water to make a smooth cream.

2. Slowly heat the milk and vanilla pod or vanilla essence in a small saucepan just to boiling point. Remove the vanilla pod, if using, then slowly whisk the milk into the egg mixture.

3. Pour the custard into the rinsed-out pan, place over a low heat and cook, stirring, until the mixture comes to the boil. Cook very gently for 2 minutes. Pour into a basin, sprinkle a little extra sugar on the top to prevent a skin forming and leave to cool. Chill.

4. Stir before using to sandwich a cake, top a pavlova or use in a pastry flan case topped with sliced fruit.

# Rich Butter Cream

Makes sufficient to fill and cover an 18 cm/7 in cake

|  | Metric | Imperial | American |
|---|---|---|---|
| Dried egg powder | 30 ml | 2 tbls | 2 tbls |
| Water | 90 ml | 6 tbls | 6 tbls |
| Caster sugar | 75 g | 3 oz | $\frac{1}{3}$ cup |
| Unsalted butter, softened | 150 g | 5 oz | $\frac{2}{3}$ cup |

**1.** Blend the dried egg and 30 ml/2 tbls of the water to a smooth cream.

**2.** Place the remaining water and sugar in a small heavy-based pan and dissolve over a low heat. Do not stir. When the sugar has dissolved, increase the temperature and boil steadily until the syrup forms a thin thread between 2 teaspoons dipped in the syrup (110°C/225°F on a sugar thermometer).

**3.** Pour the sugar syrup on to the egg mixture in a thin steady stream, whisking all the time. Continue whisking until the mixture is cool.

**4.** Gradually whisk the butter into the egg mixture, a little at a time, whisking well between each addition. Flavour as desired.

## Flavourings

***Chocolate:*** Melt 50 g/2 oz of plain chocolate and beat into the cream when cool but still liquid.

***Orange or Lemon:*** Beat in 15 ml/1 tbls of grated orange or lemon rind.

***Coffee:*** Dissolve 15 ml/1 tbls of instant coffee in 10 ml/2 tsp of boiling water and beat into the cream.

# Lemon Curd

Makes about 500 g/1 lb 2 oz

|  | Metric | Imperial | American |
|---|---|---|---|
| Lemons | 3 | 3 | 3 |
| Butter | 100 g | 4 oz | $\frac{1}{2}$ cup |
| Dried egg powder | 90 ml | 6 tbls | 6 tbls |
| Water | 90 ml | 6 tbls | 6 tbls |
| Granulated sugar | 225 g | 8 oz | 1 cup |

1. Grate the rind and squeeze the juice from the lemons. Place the butter in a bowl over a saucepan of gently simmering water and leave to melt.

2. Blend the dried egg and water to a smooth cream, stir in the lemon rind and juice. Add to the butter with the sugar.

3. Cook the curd over the gently simmering water, stirring frequently until the mixture is thick enough to coat the back of the spoon.

4. Pour the curd into small sterilised glass jars, cover with a waxed paper disc and a lid. Label and store in the refrigerator for up to 3 weeks.

## Microwave Method

Place the butter in a large bowl and melt in the microwave oven on **HIGH**. Add the sugar, lemon rind and juice blended with the dried egg and water. Stir well and cook on **DEFROST**, stirring occasionally, for 14 to 16 minutes or until the curd has thickened. Finish as above.

# Egg Nog

Serves 4

|  | Metric | Imperial | American |
|---|---|---|---|
| Dried egg powder | 45 ml | 3 tbls | 3 tbls |
| Rum or brandy | 45 ml | 3 tbls | 3 tbls |
| Water | 15 ml | 1 tbls | 1 tbls |
| Milk | 275 ml | $\frac{1}{2}$ pt | $1\frac{1}{4}$ cups |
| Can evaporated milk (175 g/6 oz) | 1 | 1 | 1 |
| Vanilla essence | 5 ml | 1 tsp | 1 tsp |
| Caster sugar | 50 g | 2 oz | $\frac{1}{4}$ cup |
| Dried egg white | 15 ml | 1 tbls | 1 tbls |
| Water | 60 ml | 4 tbls | 4 tbls |
| Grated nutmeg | | | |

1. Blend the dried egg, rum or brandy and water to a smooth cream in a basin.

2. Heat the milk, evaporated milk, vanilla essence and half the sugar to boiling point. Pour on to the dried egg mixture, whisking all the time. Strain into the rinsed-out pan.

3. Blend the egg white and 15 ml/1 tbls of the water until smooth. Stir in the remaining water and whisk until stiff. Whisk in the remaining sugar. Reheat the egg mixture, stirring all the time, but do not allow to boil.

4. Pour on to the egg whites, stirring with a wire whisk. Sprinkle generously with nutmeg. Ladle into small glasses and serve hot.

5. Alternatively, serve the egg nog chilled. After whisking the milk into the egg mixture, leave to cool, then chill. Pour the chilled mixture on to the whisked egg whites.

# Peppermint Creams

Makes 20

|  | Metric | Imperial | American |
| --- | --- | --- | --- |
| Dried egg white | 10 ml | 2 tsp | 2 tsp |
| Water | 15 ml | 1 tbls | 1 tbls |
| Single cream | 15 ml | 1 tbls | 1 tbls |
| Icing sugar | 350 g | 12 oz | 2 cups |
| A few drops of peppermint essence | | | |
| Green food colouring (optional) | | | |

1. Blend the egg white and 10 ml/2 tsp of the water until smooth. Stir in the remaining water and cream. Mix in the icing sugar and a few drops of peppermint essence and a drop of green colouring, if liked.

2. Turn on to a surface which has been dusted lightly with icing sugar and knead the paste until smooth. Roll out to 1 cm/$\frac{1}{2}$ in thickness and cut into shapes.

3. Leave the peppermint creams to harden for 1 to 2 hours then pack into boxes with waxed paper between each layer.

# Uncooked Chocolate Walnut Fudge

Makes about 900 g/2 lb

|  | Metric | Imperial | American |
|---|---|---|---|
| *Dried egg powder* | *30 ml* | *2 tbls* | *2 tbls* |
| *Water* | *60 ml* | *4 tbls* | *4 tbls* |
| *Plain chocolate* | *225 g* | *8 oz* | *½ lb* |
| *Butter* | *25 g* | *1 oz* | *2 tbls* |
| *Sweetened condensed milk* | *90 ml* | *6 tbls* | *6 tbls* |
| *Icing sugar, sifted* | *450 g* | *1 lb* | *3 cups* |
| *Vanilla essence* | *5 ml* | *1 tsp* | *1 tsp* |
| *Chopped walnuts* | *100 g* | *4 oz* | *1 cup* |

1. Butter a 20 cm/8 in square shallow tin.

2. Blend the dried egg and water to a smooth cream in a bowl. Break up and add the chocolate with the butter.

3. Place the bowl over a pan of hot water and stir briskly until the chocolate and butter have melted and the mixture is thick and creamy.

4. Add the condensed milk, icing sugar, vanilla essence and walnuts. Remove the bowl from the pan and beat the mixture until it begins to thicken.

5. Turn the fudge into the buttered tin and smooth the top. Leave to set for a few hours then cut into squares.

# Rum Truffles

Makes 12

|  | Metric | Imperial | American |
|---|---|---|---|
| Plain chocolate | 75 g | 3 oz | 3 oz |
| Butter | 15 g | $\frac{1}{2}$ oz | 1 tbls |
| Dried egg powder | 30 ml | 2 tbls | 2 tbls |
| Water | 15 ml | 1 tbls | 1 tbls |
| Rum | 15 ml | 1 tbls | 1 tbls |
| Chocolate vermicelli | 40 g | $1\frac{1}{2}$ oz | $\frac{1}{3}$ cup |

1. Break up the chocolate and place in a bowl over a pan of hot, but not boiling, water. Leave until melted. (Alternatively, place the chocolate in a bowl in a microwave oven and melt on DEFROST.) Stir in the butter.

2. Mix the egg powder, water and rum to a smooth cream. Stir into the chocolate, and beat until thickened slightly and the mixture looks a little grainy. Chill until firm enough to handle.

3. Divide the mixture into 12 equal pieces and roll into balls. Coat with the chocolate vermicelli. Place in paper petit four cases and keep cool.

# Collettes

Makes 15

|  | Metric | Imperial | American |
|---|---|---|---|
| Plain chocolate | 225 g | 8 oz | $\frac{1}{2}$ lb |
| Butter | 25 g | 1 oz | 2 tbls |
| Dried egg powder | 30 ml | 2 tbls | 2 tbls |
| Water | 15 ml | 1 tbls | 1 tbls |
| Strong black coffee | 30 ml | 2 tbls | 2 tbls |
| Dark rum | 15 ml | 1 tbls | 1 tbls |

1. Place half the chocolate in a bowl over a pan of hot, but not boiling water and stir occasionally until melted. (Alternatively, place the bowl in a microwave oven on the DEFROST setting until the chocolate has melted.)

2. Using the handle of a teaspoon, coat the inside of 15 small waxed paper petits four cases with chocolate. Make sure the coating is even and fairly thick. As each case is coated turn it upside-down on a piece of waxed paper so that top edges have an even rim. Leave to harden.

3. Melt the remaining chocolate and stir in the butter. Mix the dried egg with the water, coffee and rum to a smooth cream. Stir into the chocolate. Leave to cool.

4. When the chocolate cases are set, carefully peel off the paper cases.

5. Place the chocolate filling into a piping bag fitted with a small star meringue tube and pipe rosettes of the filling into the chocolate cases. Leave to set and place the collettes into new paper cases, if liked.

# Almond Shapes

Makes about 24

|  | Metric | Imperial | American |
|---|---|---|---|
| Almond paste (see page 105) | 1 quantity | 1 quantity | 1 quantity |
| A few drops of green food colouring | | | |
| A few drops of pink food colouring | | | |

1. Divide the almond paste into 3 equal-sized pieces. Leave one third plain and knead a few drops of green food colouring into another third and a few drops of pink food colouring into the remainder.

2. Roll out each piece of almond paste into a 15 cm/6 in square. Place the plain square over the green square and top with the pink. Roll lightly with the rolling pin to seal together.

3. Trim the edges, then cut into 2.5 cm/1 in strips. Cut the strips into oblongs or diamond shapes and place in petits four cases.

# BASICS

The recipes included in this chapter use eggs which are cooked sufficiently to be perfectly safe, but quite often we want to whip up a cake or serve a Yorkshire Pud with the Sunday roast and find that we are short of eggs. With a packet of dried in the larder or a carton of frozen in the freezer there will no longer be a need to rush out to the shops.

# Yorkshire Pudding

Serves 4 to 6

|  | Metric | Imperial | American |
|---|---|---|---|
| *Plain flour* | *100 g* | *4 oz* | *1 cup* |
| *Salt* | | | |
| *Dried egg powder* | *45 ml* | *3 tbls* | *3 tbls* |
| *Water* | *225 ml* | *8 fl oz* | *1 cup* |
| *Milk* | *150 ml* | *$\frac{1}{4}$ pt* | *$\frac{2}{3}$ cup* |
| *Melted lard or dripping* | *45 ml* | *3 tbls* | *3 tbls* |

**1.** Sift the flour, a pinch of salt and the dried egg into a bowl. Make a well in centre, add the water and mix until smooth. Beat well. Stir in the milk.

**2.** Heat the lard or dripping in a small roasting tin or individual Yorkshire pudding tins. Place in a hot oven at 230°C/450°F/Gas mark 8 for 3 minutes. Pour the batter into the tins, return to the oven and cook until risen and golden brown, about 15 to 20 minutes for small puddings, 30 minutes for a large one. Serve hot.

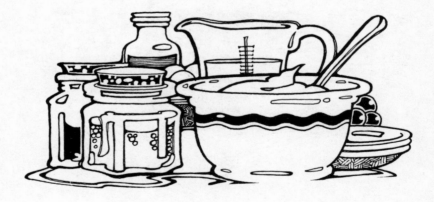

# Pancakes

Makes 8 to 10

|  | Metric | Imperial | American |
| --- | --- | --- | --- |
| *Plain flour* | *100 g* | *4 oz* | *1 cup* |
| *Dried egg powder* | *30 ml* | *2 tbls* | *2 tbls* |
| *Milk* | *275 ml* | *$\frac{1}{2}$ pt* | *$1\frac{1}{4}$ cups* |
| *Water* | *60 ml* | *4 tbls* | *4 tbls* |
| *Melted butter* | *15 ml* | *1 tbls* | *1 tbls* |
| *Oil for frying* | | | |
| *Caster sugar* | | | |
| *Lemon wedges* | | | |

1. Sift the flour and dried egg into a bowl. Gradually blend in the milk to make a smooth batter. Stir in the water and melted butter.

2. Heat a little oil in a small frying pan, then pour off into a jug, leaving the pan lightly greased. Pour in sufficient batter to coat the pan thinly and cook over a moderate heat until golden brown underneath. Turn and cook on the other side.

3. Cook the remaining pancakes in the same way. Keep the cooked pancakes hot by layering them on a plate with a piece of greaseproof paper between each. Place the plate over a pan of gently simmering water and keep the pancakes covered with a lid.

4. When all the pancakes are cooked, sprinkle with sugar and roll up. Serve with lemon wedges.

# American Pancakes

Serves 3 to 4

|  | Metric | Imperial | American |
|---|---|---|---|
| Self-raising flour | 100 g | 4 oz | 1 cup |
| Dried egg powder | 30 ml | 2 tbls | 2 tbls |
| Caster sugar | 25 g | 1 oz | 2 tbls |
| Salt | | | |
| Milk | 225 ml | 8 fl oz | 1 cup |
| Oil | 45 ml | 3 tbls | 3 tbls |
| Butter and golden syrup, honey or maple syrup to serve | | | |

1. Sift the flour and dried egg into a bowl. Add the sugar and salt. Mix the milk and oil and stir into the flour mixture. Mix just until flour is moistened, do not beat, as the batter should be lumpy.

2. Heat a large frying pan, brush with oil, then drop spoonsful of the batter on to the pan. Cook until the bubbles rise to the surface and burst and the pancakes are brown underneath. Turn and cook on the other side until golden. Keep hot while cooking the remaining batter.

3. Serve the pancakes hot with butter and honey or syrup.

# Cabinet Pudding

Serves 4 to 6

|  | Metric | Imperial | American |
|---|---|---|---|
| *Glacé cherries* | *50 g* | *2 oz* | *$\frac{1}{4}$ cup* |
| *Sponge cake crumbs* | *100 g* | *4 oz* | *2 cups* |
| *Ratafia biscuits* | *25 g* | *1 oz* | *1 oz* |
| *Chopped mixed peel* | *25 g* | *1 oz* | *$\frac{1}{4}$ cup* |
| *Dried egg powder* | *90 ml* | *6 tbls* | *6 tbls* |
| *Water* | *90 ml* | *6 tbls* | *6 tbls* |
| *Milk* | *425 ml* | *$\frac{3}{4}$ pt* | *2 cups* |
| *Caster sugar* | *25 g* | *1 oz* | *2 tbls* |
| *Vanilla essence* | *5 ml* | *1 tsp* | *1 tsp* |

1. Prepare a steamer. Place a round of greaseproof paper in the bottom of a 1.15 litre/ 2 pt/5 cup pudding basin. Grease the basin and paper.

2. Halve the cherries and arrange a few in the bottom of the basin. Mix the sponge cake crumbs with the ratafias, mixed peel and the remaining cherries. Place in the basin.

3. Blend the dried egg and water to a smooth cream. Place the milk and sugar in a saucepan and heat until the sugar dissolves. Pour on to the egg mixture, stirring all the time. Add the vanilla essence and mix well. Pour into the basin and leave to stand for 30 minutes.

4. Cover the basin with foil and place in the steamer. Steam the pudding for $1\frac{1}{2}$ hours. Turn out on to a serving plate and serve hot.

# Bread Pudding

Makes 6 portions

|  | Metric | Imperial | American |
|---|---|---|---|
| Day-old white or brown bread | 225 g | 8 oz | $\frac{1}{2}$ lb |
| Caster sugar | 25 g | 1 oz | 2 tbls |
| Sultanas | 50 g | 2 oz | $\frac{1}{3}$ cup |
| Currants | 50 g | 2 oz | $\frac{1}{3}$ cup |
| Marmalade | 30 ml | 2 tbls | 2 tbls |
| Mixed spice | 2.5 ml | $\frac{1}{2}$ tsp | $\frac{1}{2}$ tsp |
| Soft margarine | 50 g | 2 oz | $\frac{1}{4}$ cup |
| Dried egg powder | 30 ml | 2 tbls | 2 tbls |
| Water | 30 ml | 2 tbls | 2 tbls |
| Granulated sugar | 15 ml | 1 tbls | 1 tbls |

1. Tear the bread into pieces and place in a bowl. Cover with cold water and leave for 5 minutes. Squeeze the bread until almost dry, then beat until smooth.

2. Stir in the caster sugar, sultanas, currants, marmalade, spice and margarine. Blend the egg and water to a smooth cream and stir into the bread mixture. Turn into a well greased 900 ml/$1\frac{1}{2}$ pt/$3\frac{3}{4}$ cup ovenproof dish.

3. Bake in the centre of a moderate oven at 180°C/350°F/Gas mark 4 for about $1\frac{1}{4}$ hours, until firm and golden brown. Sprinkle with granulated sugar and serve warm or cold.

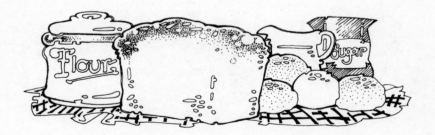

# Fruit Cake

Makes 1 × 18 cm/7 in cake

|  | Metric | Imperial | American |
|---|---|---|---|
| *Soft margarine* | *225 g* | *8 oz* | *1 cup* |
| *Caster sugar* | *225 g* | *8 oz* | *1 cup* |
| *Frozen pasteurised egg, thawed* | *175 ml* | *6 fl oz* | *¾ cup* |
| *Plain flour* | *275 g* | *10 oz* | *2½ cups* |
| *Baking powder* | *5 ml* | *1 tsp* | *1 tsp* |
| *Mixed spice* | *10 ml* | *2 tsp* | *2 tsp* |
| *Rum, brandy or orange juice* | *30 ml* | *2 tbls* | *2 tbls* |
| *Mixed dried fruit* | *450 g* | *1 lb* | *3 cups* |
| *Glacé cherries, chopped* | *50 g* | *2 oz* | *¼ cup* |

1. Cream the margarine and sugar together until pale and light. Gradually add the egg, beating well after each addition.

2. Sift the flour, baking powder and spice together and fold into the creamed mixture alternately with the rum, brandy or orange juice.

3. Mix in the dried fruit and glacé cherries. Turn the mixture into an 18 cm/7 in deep, round cake tin which has been greased and the bottom and sides lined with greased greaseproof paper.

4. Bake in the centre of a cool oven 150°C/300°F/Gas mark 2 for about 3 hours. When the cake is cooked a skewer inserted in the centre should come out clean. Remove from the tin and cool on a wire rack. Remove the paper.

# Éclairs

Makes 8

|  | Metric | Imperial | American |
| --- | --- | --- | --- |
| **Choux pastry** | | | |
| *Plain flour* | *50 g* | *2 oz* | *$\frac{1}{2}$ cup* |
| *Water* | *150 ml* | *$\frac{1}{4}$ pt* | *$\frac{2}{3}$ cup* |
| *Butter or margarine* | *25 g* | *1 oz* | *2 tbls* |
| *Frozen pasteurised egg, thawed* | *50 ml* | *2 fl oz* | *$\frac{1}{4}$ cup* |
| **Filling** | | | |
| *Double cream* | *150 ml* | *$\frac{1}{4}$ pt* | *$\frac{2}{3}$ cup* |
| **Icing** | | | |
| *Plain chocolate* | *50 g* | *2 oz* | *2 oz* |
| *Butter* | *25 g* | *1 oz* | *2 tbls* |

1. Sift the flour on to a piece of paper. Place the water and butter or margarine into a saucepan and bring to the boil. Remove from the heat and stir in the flour. Beat well. Return to a low heat and cook for a further 2 to 3 minutes, beating continuously until the mixture leaves the sides of the pan.

2. Remove from the heat and allow to cool slightly. Whisk the egg and beat into the flour mixture a little at a time.

3. Grease a baking sheet. Put the choux pastry into a piping bag fitted with a 1 cm/$\frac{1}{2}$ in plain piping tube and pipe 8 10 cm/4 in lengths on to the baking sheet.

4. Bake in the centre of a moderately hot oven at 200°C/400°F/Gas mark 6 until golden brown and crisp, about 30 minutes. Remove from the oven and slit each éclair along one side to allow the steam to escape. Leave to cool on a wire rack.

5. Whip the cream and use to fill the éclairs. Break up the chocolate and place in a bowl with the butter over a pan of hot, but not boiling, water. (Alternatively place in a microwave oven on the DEFROST setting until melted.) Stir until smooth. Spread on each éclair.

# Victoria Sandwich

Makes 1 × 18 cm/7 in cake

|  | Metric | Imperial | American |
|---|---|---|---|
| Dried egg powder | 60 ml | 4 tbls | 4 tbls |
| Water | 90 ml | 6 tbls | 6 tbls |
| Butter or margarine | 100 g | 4 oz | $\frac{1}{2}$ cup |
| Caster sugar | 100 g | 4 oz | $\frac{1}{2}$ cup |
| Self-raising flour | 100 g | 4 oz | 1 cup |
| Jam | | | |

1. Grease 2 18 cm/7 in sandwich tins, line the bases with circles of greaseproof paper and grease the paper.

2. Blend the dried egg and 60 ml/4 tbls of the water together to a smooth cream. Stir in the remaining water.

3. Cream the butter or margarine and the sugar together until light and fluffy. Gradually blend in the egg mixture, alternately with about 30 ml/2 tbls of the flour. Fold in the remaining flour.

4. Divide the cake mixture between the tins and level the tops. Bake in the centre of a moderately hot oven at 190°C/375°F/Gas mark 5 for 20 to 25 minutes. Cakes should spring back when pressed lightly with a finger and have begun to shrink from the sides of the tins.

5. Turn out the cakes on to a wire rack and remove the paper. Leave to cool. Sandwich the cakes together with jam and sprinkle a little caster sugar on the top.

# Swiss Roll

Makes 1

|  | Metric | Imperial | American |
|---|---|---|---|
| *Frozen pasteurised egg, thawed* | *100 ml* | *4 fl oz* | *½ cup* |
| *Caster sugar* | *50 g* | *2 oz* | *¼ cup* |
| *Plain flour* | *50 g* | *2 oz* | *½ cup* |
| *Baking powder* | *2.5 ml* | *½ tsp* | *½ tsp* |
| *Warmed jam* | *30 ml* | *2 tbls* | *2 tbls* |

1. Grease a 28 × 18 cm/11 × 7 in Swiss roll tin and line with greaseproof paper. Grease the paper.

2. Place the egg and sugar in a bowl. Place the bowl over a pan of gently simmering water and whisk until the mixture is light and the whisk leaves a trail when lifted. Remove the bowl from the pan and whisk the mixture until cool.

3. Sift the flour and baking powder together, and fold into the egg mixture with a metal spoon, very lightly but thoroughly. Be careful not to break down the whisked mixture. Turn into the prepared tin and shake the tin gently to level the mixture.

4. Bake in the centre of a moderately hot oven at 200°C/400°F/Gas mark 6 until risen and golden brown, about 10 minutes. When cooked, the cake should spring back when pressed lightly with a finger and have started to shrink from the sides of the tin.

5. Turn out on to a sheet of greaseproof paper which has been sprinkled generously with caster sugar. Peel off the paper from the bottom of the cake. Trim off the edges of the cake. Spread the warmed jam over the cake. Make a cut at one end of the cake about halfway through the depth of cake and 2.5 cm/1 in from the edge. Start rolling up the cake from this end, using the sugared paper to roll the cake firmly. Hold the roll in the paper for a few moments, then remove the paper and leave the cake to cool completely on a wire rack.

# INDEX OF RECIPES